CHRISTIAN HEROES: THEN & NOW

FRANCIS ASBURY

Circuit Rider

CHRISTIAN HEROES: THEN & NOW

FRANCIS ASBURY

Circuit Rider

JANET & GEOFF BENGE

P.O. BOX 55787   SEATTLE, WA 98155

YWAM Publishing is the publishing ministry of Youth With A Mission (YWAM), an international missionary organization of Christians from many denominations dedicated to presenting Jesus Christ to this generation. To this end, YWAM has focused its efforts in three main areas: (1) training and equipping believers for their part in fulfilling the Great Commission (Matthew 28:19), (2) personal evangelism, and (3) mercy ministry (medical and relief work).

For a free catalog of books and materials, call (425) 771-1153 or (800) 922-2143. Visit us online at www.ywampublishing.com.

Francis Asbury: Circuit Rider

Published by YWAM Publishing
a ministry of Youth With A Mission
P.O. Box 55787, Seattle, WA 98155-0787

This title is available as an e-book. Visit www.ywampublishing.com.

Library of Congress Cataloging-in-Publication Data

Benge, Janet, 1958–
    Francis Asbury : circuit rider / Janet and Geoff Benge.
        pages cm. — (Christian heroes, then & now)
    Includes bibliographical references.
    ISBN 978-1-57658-737-9 (pbk.)
    1. Asbury, Francis, 1745–1816—Juvenile literature. 2. Methodist Episcopal Church—Bishops—Biography—Juvenile literature. I. Benge, Geoff, 1954– II. Title.
    BX8495.A8B46 2013
    287.092—dc23
    [B]   2012048821

Unless otherwise noted, Scripture quotations are taken from the King James Version of the Bible.

First printing 2013

Printed in the United States of America

CHRISTIAN HEROES: THEN & NOW

Adoniram Judson
Amy Carmichael
Betty Greene
Brother Andrew
Cameron Townsend
Clarence Jones
Corrie ten Boom
Count Zinzendorf
C. S. Lewis
C. T. Studd
David Bussau
David Livingstone
Dietrich Bonhoeffer
D. L. Moody
Elisabeth Elliot
Eric Liddell
Florence Young
Francis Asbury
George Müller
Gladys Aylward
Hudson Taylor

Ida Scudder
Isobel Kuhn
Jacob DeShazer
Jim Elliot
John Wesley
John Williams
Jonathan Goforth
Lillian Trasher
Loren Cunningham
Lottie Moon
Mary Slessor
Nate Saint
Paul Brand
Rachel Saint
Samuel Zwemer
Rowland Bingham
Sundar Singh
Wilfred Grenfell
William Booth
William Carey

*Unit study curriculum guides
are available for select biographies.*

*Available at your local Christian
bookstore or from YWAM Publishing
1-800-922-2143 / www.ywampublishing.com*

Eastern United States

Contents

Chapter 1

Lying Low

The meeting over, Francis Asbury stood at the door of the old wooden barn where he had just preached. As he said goodbye to the men in attendance, he knew that he might never see some of these dedicated young preachers again. There was a good chance a number of them would get caught up in the war between the Patriots and the British. Nonetheless, Francis encouraged the American-born preachers to go about the business of preaching the gospel as boldly and as best they could under the circumstances.

Soon Francis was left alone with his thoughts. It was a bitter moment. The men were going off to ride circuits and preach and teach while he was holed up in a house in a remote corner of Delaware. More than anything else he wanted to be out riding the circuits. That was what he had come to the American colonies to do. For seven years he had roamed freely about the countryside, preaching and teaching and establishing Methodist Societies wherever he went. All that had changed. He was an Englishman caught in the Americans' war with the British for their independence.

Francis had been in the colonies long enough to appreciate the stand the Patriots had taken against Great Britain. He even agreed with most of their complaints. But it was the spring of 1778, and the British still occupied Philadelphia, which they had captured from Patriot forces several months before. Because of this, fear and anxiety gripped Americans living in the surrounding colonies, such as Maryland and Delaware. These Americans were unsure what the British army's next move might be. As a result, any Englishman caught riding through the countryside was immediately considered to be a Tory—an English sympathizer—and perhaps even a British spy. More than a few Englishmen had been arrested or killed.

As an Englishman, Francis found this to be a big problem. His fellow English Methodist preachers had solved the problem by getting on ships and returning home, but not Francis. He felt that God had called him to remain in America. But now he wondered whether he'd made a mistake. Perhaps he should have left for England with his best friend, George Shadford, the month before. If he had, he wouldn't be stuck in Delaware, lying low and unable to move about freely, simply because he was an Englishman. He had always been permitted to travel as a Methodist preacher, and he hoped that would never change.

Chapter 2

Apprenticed to God

Twenty-year-old Francis Asbury, or Frank as everyone called him, paced nervously up and down the living room floor. A bushel of ripe green apples sat on the table, waiting for his mother to turn them into pies, but for once that didn't bring a smile to his face. Today Frank had grim business to take care of. He took a deep breath and peered out the open window, wondering why his father was taking so long getting home from Hamstead Hall, the big estate down the road where he worked as a gardener.

His mother too—where was she? Probably praying with a neighbor, Frank decided. Ever since he was seven or eight, his mother seemed to be out praying or reading the Bible to someone nearby.

Frank stared out the window. It was dusk, and as usual the road to Birmingham, England, was busy with weary drovers guiding packhorses laden with coal. Many of the drovers would stop at the Malt House Inn and Brewery for the night, and already Frank could hear them calling to the inn boys to unload and feed their horses. The call was a sound he was familiar with, as the Asburys' two-story, redbrick cottage shared a wall with the Malt House Inn and Brewery.

Finally, his parents, Joseph and Eliza Asbury, both arrived home.

"I'm not surprised to see you here," Joseph said, shuttering the window for the night. "I assumed that you would want to have a talk now that your apprenticeship is over."

"Yes," Eliza agreed. "It's hard to believe seven years have passed and you're a tradesman now, a buckle maker no less."

Frank could hear the pride in his mother's voice. Not all the boys in their small village of Newton, located four miles outside the large industrial city of Birmingham, had the tenacity to sign up for an apprenticeship at thirteen years of age and work hard to become a tradesman in the allotted seven years.

"I suppose it's on to your own workshop now, lad?" his father said. "Your mother and I have managed to save up a little to help you start out on your own—if that's what you want to do, of course. Or you could stay with Mr. Griffin if he's asked you to. That would be alright as well."

Frank cleared his throat. "Actually, Father, I had something quite different in mind." He spoke fast, before his courage failed him. "I've decided to become a Methodist preacher—a traveling preacher."

After a long silence, just as Frank expected, his father exploded.

"A preacher? Are you out of your mind, son? How is a preacher supposed to earn his keep? You've a good trade now, one that took you seven years to learn. Surely you're not telling us you would throw all that away to gallop around on a horse preaching and praying with people. Where will that get you?"

Joseph stopped to take a breath, and Frank could see the veins in his neck pulsating. "It's wrong of those Wesley brothers to encourage the likes of you. What do they know of your situation? They are both ordained ministers with a way to make a living, but you? You'll be nothing, unrecognized by the church. You're signing on to be poor your whole life. Tell me, lad, how will you support a wife and children on the meager collections of a Methodist preacher?"

"I'm not sure, Father," Frank said. "I just know that's what God has called me to do, and I dare not go against it. The Bible tells us God will supply all our needs, and I will trust Him to do so."

"But," his father sputtered, "your apprenticeship! Why throw that away?"

Eliza spoke up. "It's true, Joseph. Frank has been apprenticed as a buckle maker these past seven years, but he has also been apprenticed to God. Now that he is a grown man, he should be free to decide which line of work to take up."

"Aye, that's what you would say, Eliza," Frank's father grumbled. "You always have favored the boy

and his strange religious leanings. Too much cod-
dling has done this to him."

The room was silent again. Frank walked toward
the door. "I do not mean to bring trouble to the
house," he said. "I just wanted you to know that I am
called by God, and I intend to follow Him."

"We understand," his mother said.

His father glared at the fireplace. "You might,
Eliza, but I don't," he retorted. "Have you thought
about your mother?" he said as he turned to Frank.
"If something happens to me, who will take care of
her if her only son is off roving around the countryside? No, boy, you have God-given responsibilities
here. Face them like a man."

Frank took a deep breath. He knew it was useless
to argue. "I need some night air," he said, opening
the door and walking out into the autumn evening.
He could smell the blackberries in the hedgerow as
he made his way across the yard to the barn, which
was in ruins now. Over the past seven years, since his
decision to become a dedicated Christian, Frank had
found the barn a place of spiritual solitude.

Frank knew that a lot of people found it hard to
understand his decision. After all, it was 1765 and
Protestant Christianity was the law of the land. British citizens were subjects of King George III, a devout
monarch who was also head of the Church of England. Yet when Frank was thirteen years old, something had happened to him that he could not fully
explain. In fact, he'd always been a sensitive child,
shaped in part by experiencing grief at a young age.

When she was five years old, Frank's only sibling, Sarah, had come down with a sudden fever and died. Frank was three at the time, but he could still remember his mother's wailing and his father lifting his sister's lifeless body into the coffin. Sarah was buried in the graveyard at St. Mary's in nearby Handsworth, and Frank accompanied his mother there many times. Eliza would sit on the grave and weep. Not only did she cry at the grave, but she would also spend hours each day at the house with her head in her hands, crying. It was all a shock to Frank. In one day he had lost his older sister and playmate along with the happy home he'd known since birth.

Frank was aware that his mother had tried everything she could think of to shake the terrible depression that had settled over her. Eliza met with the local Church of England priest and said special prayers, attended church regularly, and gave to the poor, but nothing seemed to help. However, during a visit with relatives in the nearby village of Wednesbury, Eliza had encountered a Methodist preacher who preached the Methodists' fourfold gospel: (1) All need to be saved. Every person is born with original sin and in need of redemption. (2) All can be saved. Every person in the world can be saved through the death and resurrection of Jesus Christ if he or she so chooses. (3) All can know in their hearts that they are saved. (4) All can be saved to the uttermost. That is, every Christian can grow in his or her faith to the fullest.

Hearing this message changed Eliza's life. Someone had finally explained to her how she could overcome the fear and grief she carried and know that she was saved. From that day on, Eliza Asbury was a changed woman. She became an enthusiastic Christian and spent hours each day in prayer and Bible reading. She often read aloud to Frank, who loved hearing the daring adventures of such Old Testament heroes as David and Daniel.

It was not until just before his fourteenth birthday that Frank felt the need to put his own life in God's hands. His mother had invited a traveling Baptist shoemaker to hold meetings in the Asbury home. There was something about the way this Baptist preacher spoke about God's gift of salvation that appealed to Frank. He had heard it all before, many times, but this time Frank knew he had to respond. After the meeting he went out to the barn and prayed a simple prayer, placing his life and future into God's hands.

Now, as Frank pulled open the creaking door to the old barn, he hoped that he was still following the path God had for him. His father had made many good points—points Frank had also thought about. It was true he did not have the background to make anything of himself as a Methodist preacher. The men he hoped to be like, including John and Charles Wesley and George Whitefield, were learned men who had all graduated from Oxford University. They were also ordained ministers in the Church of England. By contrast, Frank had attended several years of charity school in the neighboring hamlet of Snail's Green. His teacher had taunted him mercilessly because the

Apprenticed to God   19

Asbury home was known as a center of Methodist worship in the area. The other boys in the class
followed the teacher's lead. They called Frank "the
Methodist parson" and made fun of him because he
would not join them in swearing and fighting.

After three years at school, Frank could no longer take the taunting and left. He was able to read
and write but had little idea of any other subjects. He
hadn't traveled more than a few miles from home—
only as far as Wednesbury, three miles to the west,
and occasionally south to Birmingham. It was certainly not the kind of traveling that would prepare
him to become a Methodist circuit rider, going great
distances on horseback to preach the gospel from village to village around England.

The Methodists were not a church but were an
evangelical community within the Church of England known for their disciplined lives. Methodist
preachers openly preached to any crowd that gathered, but to be a member of a Methodist Society, a
person had to attend meetings regularly, be accountable to his or her leader, give money, study the Bible,
and pray every day. The Methodist band leaders and
preachers issued "tickets" of good standing to members. These tickets, valid for three months, gave the
person entry to Methodist Society meetings. At the
end of the three months, each society member had to
apply for a new ticket by proving that he was carefully following the ways and practices of the society.

As Frank sat on an old barrel in the barn, he considered the phrase his mother had used: "apprenticed

to God." Yes, he decided, it fit well. In the seven years he had worked as an apprentice buckle maker for Mr. Griffin, he had also been undergoing a kind of religious apprenticeship. Through the meetings at his home and Methodist meetings in nearby Wednesbury, he had been introduced to some of the leading Christian men in the area. He had been attracted by the strange, new experience of seeing grown men and women who seemed to have a direct connection to God: they preached without sermon notes, sang songs without a hymnal, and prayed spontaneous prayers rather than read them from the authorized prayer book. Over time, men like John Ryland, a Church of England curate and leading Methodist from Birmingham, took a particular interest in Frank. John loaned him books and gave him Christian advice. Another rising star in the Methodist movement, Edward Stillingfleet, also acted as Frank's mentor and spiritual guide. He provided Frank with a steady supply of books and sermons, which Frank read and took notes on. Although he had not gone beyond elementary school, Frank had managed to educate himself far beyond that level.

By the time Frank was seventeen, he was taking his turn preaching at some of the smaller Methodist meetings in the surrounding area. His employer, Mr. Griffin, allowed him to have Sundays off. This was a particularly busy day for Frank, who, with four other devout young men from around the Great Barr area, formed what Methodists called a band. A band was a group of either men or women who agreed to meet together weekly for prayer, confession, singing, and spiritual encouragement. There were five young men in Frank's band: Thomas Ault, a shoemaker's apprentice and Frank's closest friend; James Mayo; James Bayley, a park keeper; and Thomas Russell, a carpenter's apprentice. The group would meet together early on Sunday mornings.

Frank quickly became the leader of his band, and as such he was expected to start each weekly meeting by asking all in the group a number of prescribed questions:

1. Have you the forgiveness of your sins?
2. Have you peace with God through our Lord Jesus Christ?
3. Have you the witness of God's Spirit with your spirit that you are a child of God?
4. Is the love of God shed abroad in your heart?
5. Has no sin, inward or outward, dominion over you?
6. Do you desire to be told of your faults?
7. Do you desire that every one of us should tell you, from time to time, whatsoever is in his heart concerning you?
8. Consider! Do you desire we should tell you whatsoever we think, whatsoever we fear, whatsoever we hear, concerning you?
9. Do you desire that, in doing this, we should come as close as possible, that we should cut to the quick and search your heart to the bottom?

10. Is it your desire and design to be on this, and all other occasions, entirely open, so as to speak everything that is in your heart without exception, without disguise, and without reserve?

When each band member had taken his turn answering the questions, the members would all pray for each other's spiritual well-being. They would then walk to the village of Wednesbury, where they would conduct an 8:00 a.m. meeting with the Methodist Society. After this meeting they would walk on to West Bromwich to preach at two meetings before returning to Wednesbury to preach at the 5:00 p.m. meeting. In all, it was a twelve-mile circuit that provided an opportunity for any member of the band who wanted to preach, and Frank was always ready and eager to volunteer.

When he turned nineteen years old, Frank volunteered to become a local preacher. In addition to holding this unpaid job, he had to fulfill all his apprenticeship obligations to Mr. Griffin. Every minute of Frank's life was soon accounted for. He awoke at four o'clock each morning to get his work done early. Later in the day, usually around midafternoon, Frank would walk as far as Derbyshire, Staffordshire, Warwickshire, or Worcestershire to preach and talk with people who needed to hear about God's love and mercy. Then he would walk home again, often not falling into bed until midnight or later. Then it was up again at 4:00 a.m. Frank followed this schedule four or five days a week, every week, and also kept up his busy Sunday schedule. As he walked from village to village, he would sing the hymns written by Charles Wesley. He wished he had a horse, not because it would make the trip faster, but because he'd heard that John Wesley could ride and read his Bible in the saddle, and Frank longed for more time for Bible study and meditation. He was always painfully aware of his basic education.

Now, at twenty years of age, Frank knew that God was calling him to give his life to preaching and teaching. Yet his father was right: he was poorly equipped to do so. He could not think of anything else to do but pray about the situation. He knelt down in the old barn. *God, You know my heart*, he began. *You know that I want to follow You and tell others how to find the same peace in their hearts as You have given me. Whatever happens next, I am Your servant and in Your hands. Amen.*

When Frank stood up, he felt much better. He knew he had to go back into the house and face his father, but somehow that did not matter. It was much more important to please his heavenly Father, and that path meant leaving buckle making behind and venturing out into the highways and byways of the English countryside.

As he strolled back across the yard to the house, Frank hummed the words of one of Charles Wesley's hymns: "My chains fell off, my heart was free / I rose, went forth, and followed Thee."

Chapter 3

Who Among You
Is Willing to Go?

In early 1766, Frank set out on horseback to begin riding his first Methodist circuit between Staffordshire, to the north of Birmingham, and Gloucester to the south. He was ready and determined to become a worthy Methodist preacher. It had not been easy disentangling himself from his parents. He didn't expect his father's support, but his mother's reaction had surprised him. She pressed him to stay close to home and out of danger. "You are the only child I have," she told Frank, reminding him of the grief she endured when his sister died. "You don't remember the Wesley riots here, but I do. Your father and I were newly married, and John Wesley came through the area. He preached not five miles from here at West Bromwich. The local vicar rode through the listeners, yelling curses at them and determined to trample them with his horse. What if that should happen again?"

Frank considered his mother's words. Fellow band member Thomas Ault had told him how his family had moved to Newton from West Bromwich after their house was looted and burned in the anti-Methodist riots that occurred there in 1745, the year Frank was born. The truth was that Methodist preachers, such as Frank aspired to be, often preached in places where more "proper" Church of England vicars would not go. John and Charles Wesley led by example, preaching in coal-mining pits, outside public houses, in graveyards, and anywhere people would gather to listen. Many times there was loud and sometimes violent opposition from locals to the message being preached. Like the Wesley brothers, Frank was not going to let opposition stop him from preaching the gospel—even if he had to risk a riot.

Despite his mother's concerns, Frank quickly adjusted to his new life as a circuit rider, which involved much preaching, praying, Bible reading, and staying with Christians from all walks of life. As he rode his circuit, he tried to write regularly to his parents. In one of his letters to them he declared that he would "rather be in the saddle than in a seat in the House of Lords."

The more he traveled, preached, and met with various bands, the more enthusiastic Frank became about the advantages of the Methodist way. The name

Methodist accurately described the life he would now live. The term was first applied to John and Charles Wesley and George Whitefield while they were studying to become Church of England clergymen at Oxford University during the early 1730s. The Wesleys' mother, Susannah, had nineteen children, and to cope with such a large family she had operated with strict routines, including regulating her children's spiritual lives. Drawing on this background, the three young vicars-in-training looked for methods that would help Christians become holy and useful to God. It wasn't long before they came up with a set of rules and routines for Christians to follow and ways for them to be accountable to each other. Because of this, people began mockingly calling the Wesley brothers and George Whitefield *Methodists*— people who relied on methods to promote holiness.

Now, more than thirty years later, no follower of the Wesleys was left with any doubt as to how or when to worship. Every aspect of a Methodist's life was regulated. Methodists were expected to rise early and devote the first hour of the day to prayer and follow many other rules. Members were also held accountable for their actions.

As a circuit-riding Methodist preacher, Frank was held to an even higher standard. He was required to rise at 4:00 a.m. on days when he was going to preach and 5:00 a.m. on other days. Like all other Methodists, he spent the first hour in prayer and another hour each morning reading and meditating on verses from the Bible.

Frank's main job as a circuit rider, apart from preaching, was to meet with the Methodist band leaders on his circuit, praying with them and inquiring as to the state of their spiritual well-being. He would lead each band leader through the same set of questions the members of the band back home in Newton had been asked. Frank would take notes on the answers given and discuss spiritual and other challenges the band leaders faced.

Besides being responsible for making sure that the Methodist Society members on his circuit were following the ways and practices of the society, Frank had his own personal list of things to do while riding between one society band and the next. John Wesley had made it clear to his preachers that they were to never waste a second of time. They were to memorize scriptures—along with Methodist sermons and hymns—as their horses clopped along the country lanes.

Frank worked hard at mastering the songs found in the Methodist hymnbook tucked in his saddlebags. Charles Wesley was a gifted hymn writer whose songs, some said, were destined to be sung for a hundred years. Since so many members of Methodist Societies could not read or write, Frank and other preachers taught them the words to Charles's hymns to instill Methodist teaching. At the front of the hymnal were instructions for how those at a Methodist Society meeting should sing:

Sing *all*. Let not a slight degree of weakness or weariness hinder you. If it is a cross to you, take it up and you will find it a blessing.

Sing *lustily* and with good courage. Beware of singing as if you are half dead or half asleep, but lift up your voice with strength. Be no more afraid of your voice now, nor more ashamed of being heard, than when you sing the songs of Satan.

Sing *modestly*. Strive to unite your voices together so as to make one clean melodious sound.

Sing in *tune*, and take care not to sing too slow. This drawling way naturally steals on all who are lazy; and it is high time to drive it from among us, and sing all our tunes just as quick as we did at first.

Above all sing *spiritually*. Have an eye to God in every word you sing. Attend strictly to the sense of what you sing, and see that your heart is not carried away with the sound, but offered to God continually.

As he rode his circuit, Frank encountered opposition to his preaching, especially when he preached in the coal-mining towns. Life in the mining towns was hard. The mines were dangerous places to work. Frequent accidents left miners dead or disabled. Young children were put to work opening and shutting trapdoors to let coal carts through or pushing the heavy carts. The mines were dark and damp, and it was not unusual for those working below to be wading in thigh-deep water. Everything about coal mining

was grim, and it seemed to Frank that the black coal
dust that settled over the mining towns also settled
in the souls of those who lived in them. Coal miners often used gin as a way to escape the grimness of
their everyday lives, and they seemed to be angry at
anyone—especially someone from out of town—who
suggested they pour out their alcohol and replace it
with Bible reading and prayer.

Still, Frank did not give up. He recalled the words
of John Wesley: "You have nothing to do but to save
souls. Therefore spend and be spent in this work.
Gaining knowledge is a good thing, but saving souls
is better." As Frank rode from town to town preaching, he comforted himself with Wesley's words. He
was determined to keep doing God's work as long as
he had the strength.

Soon the leaders of the Methodist Society recognized Frank's determination and discipline. In 1768
Frank was given a new circuit in Bedfordshire and
Sussex, closer to London. The following year he was
appointed to Northamptonshire, northwest of Bedfordshire, and then to Salisbury in Wiltshire in the
southwest of England.

While riding these new circuits, Frank was too far
away to see his parents on a regular basis. He had
to be content to send them letters that were often
passed along a network of Methodist circuit riders
to get to their destination. He heard from others that
his mother was having a difficult time adjusting to
his being so far from home. Immediately he wrote
to her. "I hope, my dear mother, that you are more

easy. Why will you mourn in such a manner? If you have given me to the Lord, let it be a free will offering and don't grieve for me. As for me, I know what I am called to. It is to give up all I have, my hands and heart in the work, yea, the nearest and dearest friends. And I am content and will do it. Nay, it is done. Christ is all to me. I love my parents and friends, but I love my God better and His service, because it is perfect freedom, and He does not send me to warfare at my own cost . . . and though I have given up all, I do not repent, for I have found all."

Although Frank enjoyed what he was doing as a circuit rider, even when he was heckled, he felt confined. He longed to preach the gospel to a new group of people, those who lived far away from the nearest church. Britain, deeply rooted in the traditions of the Church of England, did not provide this opportunity, but he knew of somewhere that did—the American colonies.

Even though he had not met them, Frank closely followed the lives of Joseph Pilmore and Richard Boardman, two young Methodist preachers who had been sent to the American colonies two years before. Their letters home were circulated within the societies, and Frank had devoured them.

The more Frank read these letters, the more he felt that God was leading him to cross the Atlantic Ocean. He knew that any kind of missionary work would be difficult, but the American colonies presented specific challenges. Every week there seemed to be more news of unrest in the colonies over King

George III's determination to collect a series of taxes from the colonists. He wanted these revenues to pay the war debt incurred fighting with France over control of Canada. Those living in the thirteen American colonies did not want to pay these taxes to Great Britain, and the year before, British troops had fired on a mob of protesters during the Boston Massacre. Five colonists were killed, and the British government was forced to back down. The Sugar Tax and Stamp Act were repealed, but the tax on tea was left in place. Even though there had been no recent news of clashes between the colonists and British troops, most people expected more trouble to erupt. Despite this unsettled situation, Frank felt drawn to the American colonies.

In summer of 1771, Frank attended his first Methodist Preachers' Conference. The event was being held in Bristol, a bustling port city in southwest England which Frank had never visited. As he traveled to Bristol, he took every opportunity to visit the many Methodist bands located in the villages and towns he passed through. As he rode, Frank spent many hours praying about his future.

Frank arrived in Bristol, England's fourth-largest city, on August 1, 1771, and made his way to the New Room, the Methodist meetinghouse located in central Bristol. Over one hundred Methodist preachers were gathered, and at first Frank was overcome, seeing so many dedicated men together in one place. He had spent so much of the past five years riding alone along country lanes and meeting with small groups of believers that he felt overwhelmed to be surrounded by so many other Methodist preachers.

Following a hearty meal, Frank took a tour of the legendary meetinghouse. The building was the first Methodist chapel, having been built thirty-two years before in 1739. Frank loved the simple wooden pews made from reclaimed ship lumber and the two-tiered pulpit that allowed the preacher to stand close to the congregation on the ground floor or higher up if the balcony was filled with listeners. He also saw John Wesley's living quarters upstairs, as well as a day school, bookstall, and pharmacy for the poor.

Frank found board with a local Methodist family, and that evening all of the preachers gathered to hear John Wesley preach. It was a meeting Frank would never forget. John was sixty-eight years old, yet he was as sprightly as a man half his age. His hair was completely white, but his back was straight and his voice rang out across the pews. Frank listened carefully to his words:

> And he said to them all, "If any man will come after me, let him deny himself, and take up his cross daily, and follow me" (Luke 9:23).
>
>   It has been frequently imagined that the direction here given is related chiefly, if not wholly, to the Apostles, at least, to the Christians of the first ages, or those in a state of persecution. But this is a grievous mistake; for although our blessed Lord is here directing his discourse more immediately to his Apostles, and those other disciples who attended him in

the days of his flesh, yet in them he speaks to us, and to all mankind, without any exception or limitation. The meaning is, "If any man," of whatever rank, station, circumstances, in any nation, in any age of the world, "will" effectually "come after me, let him deny himself" in all things; let him "take up his cross" of whatever kind; yea, and that "daily, and follow me."

If we are not walking in the way of the cross, we are not following Him; we are not treading in his steps but going back from, or at least wide of, Him.

Frank was enthralled listening to John Wesley. It was just the message he needed to hear. Frank knew he was a gardener's son and a buckle maker by trade, but he was still "any man," and John's sermon assured him that he could play as great a role in spreading the gospel as anyone else.

During one of the final meetings of the conference John spoke about his concerns for the British colonists in America. Some Methodists from England and Ireland had emigrated to the New World and taken their Methodist practices with them. John mentioned three of these men in particular: Robert Strawbridge, an Irish farmer who held meetings in his home in Maryland; Captain Thomas Webb, who had gone to America with the British army and fought with General James Wolfe in the French and Indian Wars; and Philip Embury, an Irish-German carpenter. Richard Boardman and Joseph Pilmore had joined these men, and together they worked to set up a network

of Methodist Societies around New York and Philadelphia. But as John explained, much more had to be
done. The Methodists in America were begging for
help. John then drew a deep breath and concluded
his address: "The harvest is ripe but the laborers are
few," he intoned. "Our brothers in America call aloud
for help. There are now over two and a half million
citizens living in the colonies. Who among you is
willing to go over there and help them? Who among
you will say to God, 'Here I am, send me'?"

Frank felt his heart beat fast. At that moment he
was certain God was calling him, asking him to give up
his ties to his homeland and set out across the Atlantic
Ocean. He did not hesitate to stand when John asked
preachers to walk forward if they felt God was calling
them to the colonies. Four other men also stepped out
into the aisle and made their way to the front.

The following day, John and the Methodist elders
interviewed all five of the men. Two of the elders
questioned Frank's age—he was twenty-six years
old—wondering whether he was mature enough to
be entrusted with taking the Methodist message so
far away. Would he have the experience and tact to
deal with the difficult situations that were bound
to arise? Frank replied that he did not know, but
he knew that God had called him to America. John
nodded in approval at the response. Eventually two
of the volunteers were chosen to make the journey.
Francis Asbury was one of them.

As soon as the conference in Bristol was over,
Frank hurried northward to Newton, hoping to get

home before someone else broke the news to his parents. He dreaded what they would say. He arrived home in record time, before the news reached the household. He wasted no time in telling his mother and father of his new calling in life. Just as he expected, his parents were devastated by the news.

"But we hardly heard from you when you were circuit riding in England. How will I know you are safe in America?" his mother asked.

His father shook his head. "It's a sad thing when a man's God directs him to leave his mother and father to die alone. Don't you think you might be mistaken, lad?"

"I will be back in four years," Frank replied. "Many people cross back and forth to America."

"Nay, lad," his father said. "If you go, we will never see you again."

Frank did not have an answer for this, other than to remind his parents that God had called him to go.

Later that week, Frank's mother received a letter from a group of Methodist women at Whitchurch, where Frank had often preached. Eliza read the letter aloud to him, her voice catching several times as she did so.

Dear Mrs. Asbury,

We have heard that your son is going, or has gone, to America. We expected he would call on us, to bid us farewell. But as the time is expired, we must give up our hope.

So we have troubled you with a few lines, by way of inquiring if you were willing to part with him, and he willing to part from you. We think it must be an instance of much trouble to both, for indeed we were very much grieved when we heard Mr. Asbury was going there. The intent of writing this is to beg the favor of you to send us a few lines, as soon as possible, that we many be informed of the particulars of this long journey, if he is gone; for we scarce believe he is so mad, and to desire another letter from you the first time he writes to you from abroad.

After she had read the letter, Eliza broke down, sobbing yet again. Frank realized that it was time for him to be on his way. The longer he stayed at home, the more depressing it was becoming for all of them. On August 28, 1771, he said a final goodbye to his parents.

Frank's father and mother both clung to him as he packed his saddlebags with books. Even Joseph broke down and wept. Frank was shocked. He could not recall his father ever showing such emotion. His mother cried as well, and he felt terrible. Before he mounted his horse to leave, he pulled out his silver pocket watch—the only valuable thing he owned—and thrust it into his mother's hands. Then, sobbing loudly himself, he slung his leg over the saddle, grabbed the reins tightly, and galloped away. The final words of his father rang in his ears as he departed: "We'll never see each other again. I know it."

Chapter 4

Suspended Between Two Worlds

It was Wednesday, September 4, 1771, a hot summer's day, when Francis Asbury and Richard Wright stepped aboard a three-masted schooner resting on the mud in Pill Harbor on the Avon River near Bristol.

"Don't worry about the mud, men," Captain Hood said cheerfully as he welcomed them aboard. "Nothing to worry about. The river mouth here does strange things. The tide can rise and fall forty feet, nothing else quite like it in the world far as I know. The tide turned an hour ago. Give it four hours, and the ship will be floating high enough for the hobblers to drag her down to the river mouth."

Frank nodded and smiled. He didn't really understand much of what the captain said. Time and tides
were confusing to a person who had seldom seen the
sea, but he trusted that Captain Hood knew what he
was talking about.

Once aboard, Frank and Richard carried their
bags below deck, where they shared a cabin. Frank
was grateful he had anything at all to carry aboard.
He had arrived back in Bristol without a penny, and
the members of the Methodist Society there had taken
it upon themselves to outfit him for his time in the
American colonies. The group had taken up offerings
and told Frank and Richard not to worry about their
bedding for the voyage; it would all be taken care of.
And it had. At the last meeting of the society, Frank
and Richard had been presented with ten pounds
each, a change of clothes, and blankets. The only
other things Frank had with him were some paper
and ink and a pile of books that included *The Work of
God in New England* by Jonathan Edwards, *Pilgrim's
Progress* by John Bunyan, some of John Wesley's dia-
ries and sermons, and of course his Bible. Frank and
Richard also carried with them a large pulpit Bible (a
gift from the Methodists of Bristol to their brethren
in Philadelphia), twenty pounds, and a collection of
books for the Methodists in New York.

The cabin Frank would be sharing with Richard
was low and cramped and did not contain beds.
Frank's heart sank when he realized he should have
brought a cot with him. Now he would have to spend
the entire voyage lying on bare floorboards with just

two blankets to cushion his body as the vessel rolled around. On deck above them, he could hear the crew readying the ship for the fifty- to sixty-day voyage across the Atlantic Ocean. Barrels were being rolled around, and wooden crates were being lowered into the ship's hold with ropes.

By midafternoon, just as Captain Hood had said, the tide had come in and the vessel now floated at its mooring. Teams of men lined up on each side of the Avon River. As the tide turned, sailors threw ropes to the men. The lines were attached to the ship's bow, and on deck someone shouted, "Heave-ho!" Frank watched as the men on the riverbank began pulling on the ropes. The ship then moved away from its mooring and headed downriver.

"Those men on the riverbank are called hobblers," Richard told Frank. "Captain Hood says they all come from Pill and have been pulling ships the four miles downriver to the channel for generations. Of course, the outgoing tide helps move the ship along."

"Oh," Frank replied, hardly hearing what his traveling companion was saying. His mind was on the sermon he had preached the night before at the meetinghouse in Bristol. He had chosen Psalm 61:1–2 as the text for his message: "Hear my cry, O God; attend unto my prayer. From the end of the earth will I cry unto thee, when my heart is overwhelmed: lead me to the rock that is higher than I." He repeated the verses to himself, feeling overwhelmed at what he was leaving behind and the unknown life that awaited him.

Once the tide and the hobblers had done their work, the ship drifted out of the mouth of the Avon River and into the Bristol Channel. Captain Hood gave the order to hoist the sails, and the crew jumped into action, climbing the masts and unfurling them.

Frank watched as the wind filled the sails and the ship began moving down the Bristol Channel. He felt his body sway with each swell the ship passed through. Suddenly his mouth became dry, his head pounded, and he leaned over the side of the ship and vomited. He hoped that would make him feel better, but instead he felt worse, much worse. He staggered below deck to his cabin and collapsed onto the blankets. As the ship rose and fell time and time again, Frank felt the sickest he had in his entire life. He longed for fresh air, but he could not imagine standing up and making his way up the ladder to the deck. Instead he just lay on the cabin floor. From time to time he opened his eyes and glanced up at the books he had brought with him, wondering whether he would ever feel well enough to read them.

Four days later Frank ventured back up on deck. By now the ship had passed through the Bristol Channel and rounded southern Ireland and was sailing in the open water of the Atlantic Ocean. Frank breathed in the salty air and stared at the vast expanse of surging gray water around him. He felt like a man suspended between two worlds. For better or for worse, he was on his way to a new life in the New World.

Later in the afternoon Frank felt strong enough to unpack his writing gear. From a small wooden box he pulled a quill pen and a bottle of black ink. Before Frank had left Bristol, John Wesley had urged him to keep a diary. Frank had intended to start the diary the day he set foot aboard ship, but his bout of seasickness had kept him from it. Now he sat in his cabin, legs braced against the wall, and wrote his thoughts into a leatherbound journal:

Thursday, September 12. I will set down a few things that lie on my mind. Whither am I going? To the New World. What to do? To gain honor? No, if I know my own heart. To get money? No; I am going to live to God, and to bring others so to do.

In America there has been a work of God, some moving first amongst the Friends [Quakers] but in time it declined, likewise by the Presbyterians, but amongst them also it declined. The people God owns in England are the Methodists. The doctrines they preach and the discipline they enforce are, I believe, the purest of any people now in the world.

That Sunday, Frank preached to the passengers and sailors. No one responded to his message, but he was not discouraged. There would be at least six more Sundays on which to preach before they once again saw land.

When storms arose and the ship bobbed like a cork on the ocean, Frank comforted himself with words from John Wesley's diary. Thirty-six years before, the Wesley brothers had come to America themselves. They had left from Gravesend on the River Thames, bound for the three-year-old Georgia colony with Governor James Oglethorpe. John was engaged to be the Church of England minister to the colony, and his brother Charles was to be Governor Oglethorpe's personal secretary. The voyage out had changed John's life and the Methodist movement. Reading about the storm and how John had met the Moravians aboard ship was now more real than ever to Frank. Frank could just imagine John struggling along the passageway to visit the twenty-five Moravian Christians. He reread John's account of the incident:

> In the midst of the psalm wherein their service began, the sea broke over, split the mainsail to pieces, covered the ship, and poured in between the decks, as if the great deep had already swallowed us up. A terrible screaming began among the English. The Germans looked up, and without intermission calmly sang on. I asked one of them afterward, "Was [sic] you not afraid?" He answered, "I thank God, no." I asked, "But were not your women and children afraid?" He replied mildly, "No, our women and children are not afraid to die."

Frank recalled how, at the Methodist preachers conference in Bristol the month before, John had described this encounter on the ship as one of the most meaningful of his life. It showed him that although he had all the trappings and disciplines of the Christian life, he lacked the inner peace that the Moravians possessed. The rest of John and Charles Wesley's time in Georgia was a dismal failure. The brothers were too strict and rigid for the colonists, and John was forbidden to evangelize among the Native Americans as he had hoped to do. Charles returned to England almost immediately, and John lasted only a year and a half before he also returned, discouraged and humbled. However, back in England, John sought out a group of Moravian Christians, through whom he found the peace he was looking for.

And now Frank was headed westward to the American colonies himself. He wrote in his own journal:

> The wind blowing a gale, the ship turned up and down and from side to side, in a manner very painful to one that was not accustomed to sailing; but when Jesus is in the ship all is well. Oh, what would not one do, what would he not suffer, to be useful to souls and to the will of his great Master! Lord, help me to give thee my heart now and forever. . . . I feel my spirit bound to the New World and my heart united to the people, though unknown, and have great cause to believe that I am not running before I am sent. The more troubles I meet with, the more convinced I am that I am doing the will of God.

As the weeks of the journey across the Atlantic passed, Frank and Richard took turns preaching on

Sunday mornings. Many passengers and sailors listened to what they had to say, but none were converted. On October 13, thirty-nine days into the voyage, Frank had to stand with his back against the mizzenmast to steady himself as he preached. He spoke about being reconciled to God, and afterward he confided in his journal:

> I felt the power of truth in my own soul, but still, alas! saw no visible fruit; but my witness is in heaven, that I have not shunned to declare to them all the counsel of God. Many have been my trials in the course of this voyage, from the want of a proper bed and proper provisions, from sickness, and from being surrounded with men and women ignorant of God and very wicked. But all this is nothing. If I cannot bear this, what have I learned? Oh, I have reason to be much ashamed of many things, which I speak and do before God and man. Lord, pardon my manifold defects and failures in duty.

Two weeks later, on Sunday, October 27, Frank heard the words he'd been waiting for. A sailor in the crow's nest yelled, "Land ho!" Frank rushed up on deck, his long blond hair whipping in the wind, to catch his first glimpse of the New World. On the horizon lay a strip of land. As the hours passed and the ship inched closer to shore, the strip grew into a lush green cape.

"That's Cape May," Captain Hood said before Frank even had time to ask what it was called. "And there in the distance to port is Cape Henlopen."

The ship slowly made her way through the gap between the two capes into Delaware Bay.

"Not too long to go now. On up the river and we'll be at Philadelphia," Captain Hood assured the two Methodist men.

As the ship began making its way up the Delaware River, Frank stood on deck and watched birds skim low in flight across the broad river. Amid the brown, orange, and red foliage at the river's edge, he could see deer foraging. When the ship rounded a bend in the lower Delaware River, there, in full view, was the Philadelphia skyline.

"Quite a sight, isn't it?" Captain Hood remarked. "Philadelphia is the largest port city in North America, and growing all the time. I think the population of the city is about twenty-eight thousand now. The Scottish, Irish, and Germans outnumber the Quakers, but it's still a Quaker town. You can see that in the buildings."

Frank nodded as he noted the plain, solid, red-brick warehouses that lined the shore. Philadelphia was certainly a bustling place. Ships were tied up at docks along the edge of the river, and crews were busy loading and unloading them. Before long, Frank's ship was moored at one of the wooden docks, and the crew was preparing to unload all the barrels and crates.

Frank was glad when it came time to disembark. He followed Richard down the gangway onto the dock. It felt good to have his feet on land once again—land that did not pitch and roll. But even though the land Frank was standing on was solid, he found himself still swaying when he tried to walk, as if he were still aboard ship.

"Sea legs," Frank heard the voice of Captain Hood from behind him. He turned to see the captain walking along the dock, his arms filled with bundles of mail and other papers. "It takes a day or so to get used to walking in a straight line with nothing moving under you," the captain explained.

Captain Hood was on his way to the London Coffeehouse. He explained to Frank and Richard that the coffeehouses of Philadelphia dominated the official and social life of the city. The coffeehouses were the regular meeting places of Quaker municipal officers, ship captains, and local merchants. Whenever he arrived in Philadelphia, Captain Hood first went to the London Coffeehouse to deliver mail and try to get a good price for his cargo. "You should make it a point to acquaint yourselves with the coffeehouses while you are in Philadelphia," the captain encouraged Frank and Richard. "A very fine way to pass an hour or two."

Sea legs or not, Frank was eager to find his way to the home of Francis Harris, whose address was written on a note tucked inside Frank's Bible. Francis was a prosperous Methodist man who hosted Methodists passing through Philadelphia. John Wesley had sent him a letter telling him to expect Frank and Richard. Frank hoped he had received it.

A New World

As Frank and Richard made their way along the crowded dock, they passed ships flying flags from Hispaniola, Cuba, and other Caribbean islands. One vessel even flew a flag from faraway China. Everybody they passed seemed to be busy loading or unloading wagons and handcarts, while colonial women in fancy dresses hurried past sailors about to set out on dangerous voyages. Children, some bound for boarding schools in England and Europe, wept as they were parted from their parents.

Another sight caught Frank's attention: African slaves carrying heavy boxes on their heads. In England, some fourteen thousand slaves lived and served in their masters' great country homes. They did not work in the fields as Frank had been told they did in the American colonies. Frank had heard about the vast number of slaves in the colonies and knew that some people considered them essential to the economy. But he could not shake the idea that a slave had a soul and aspirations just like any free white person.

As Frank and Richard turned a corner and headed away from the river, Frank was awestruck. The size of the buildings was remarkable, and church spires could be seen all over the town. He had just disembarked in the second largest English-speaking city in the world, and since he had never been to London, this was the biggest city he had ever been in. He was particularly impressed by the way Philadelphia was laid out in a grid system, with broad streets that crossed each other at right angles. He recalled hearing that William Penn had designed it this way when he founded it eighty-nine years before. The grid system made it easy for Frank and Richard to find their way to the home of Francis Harris, where the two men received a warm welcome. Francis embraced them both and showed them to their room on the second floor. As Frank looked around his host's house, he was surprised to see that it was as modern and spacious as any house he'd visited in England.

A hot meal was prepared for the men. Frank looked forward to fresh meat and vegetables and food that hadn't been prepared in a ship's galley.

"It's off to St. George's tonight," Francis announced as they began the meal. "No doubt you've heard it spoken of often enough. Joseph Pilmore will be preaching. Everyone will be glad to see you and hear news from home. I hope you have plenty of that!"

Frank nodded. "And a pulpit Bible from the Reverend John Wesley, which I am to present to Brother Pilmore," he added.

"Wonderful," Francis said. "You men are in for a surprise. Most people who come here from England assume that we are all backward, but St. George's would rival any Methodist chapel back there. And how we got it is nothing short of a miracle."

"How so?" Frank asked, pausing between mouthfuls of delicious beef stew.

"It's quite a story," Francis said, pulling out his pocket watch and glancing at it, "but I think I've time to tell it. The land where St. George's sits—and that was to be its intended name—was bought by a German Reformed congregation, who started building the church. As it turned out, they overreached and stretched their money too thinly. They borrowed two thousand pounds to build the church and ran out of money before it was outfitted inside. It was a terrible thing, really."

Francis paused to shake his head and take a bite of his dinner. "Anyway," he continued, "the Germans weren't able to raise any more money, and their creditors insisted that the unfinished church be auctioned off. Some of the Germans who signed the note to borrow the money were put in debtor's prison. Now here's where it gets interesting," he said, leaning forward. "A young man from a wealthy family was walking by the auction and for some unknown reason, though I would say it was God's providence, bid 650 pounds for it. He won the bid and then told the auctioneer that his father would pay the bill. The young man's father was furious. Privately he told his friends that he thought his son suffered from bouts of insanity. That aside, what could be done with a large church building? To save face, the father asked around and found that the Methodists would be willing to pay five hundred pounds to take the church building off his hands, which we did. In the end we got a two-thousand-pound building for a quarter of its price!"

"Astonishing," Frank agreed. "Was there a vibrant Methodist Society here at the time?"

Francis nodded. "Ah, you have not met Captain Thomas Webb yet. I hope you will soon. I believe he has just left to return to New York. Captain Webb is a retired British army officer. He has only one eye and wears a patch over the other, yet he is one of the most powerful preachers the colonies have ever heard. He came to Philadelphia in 1767 to stir up a handful of Methodists converted under the great George White-field back in the 1730s. They were meeting in a rigging loft in Dock Street when Captain Webb arrived."

After stopping to chuckle, Francis continued. "What a preacher the man is. He always wears his Redcoat uniform and starts every sermon by unsheathing his sword and laying it across the pulpit. That quickly gets everyone's attention. Within two years of Captain Webb's arrival, one hundred people were in the Methodist Society, and they'd outgrown the rigging loft. That's why it was such a blessing to get the German church. We had just moved into it when Joseph Pilmore and Richard Boardman arrived. I think it surprised them to see we were that organized. And we've continued to grow since then. You'll meet a lot of them tonight, I have no doubt."

During the remainder of the meal, Frank and Richard quizzed their host on the number and types of churches in Philadelphia and the number of Methodist preachers working in the outlying areas.

Frank was happy to learn that Francis had traveled with Captain Webb into the small villages around Delaware and Pennsylvania, preaching and encouraging small groups of Methodists.

That night, just as Francis had predicted, the two missionary arrivals from England received a warm welcome at St. George's. Before going to bed, Frank wrote in his journal:

> The people looked on us with pleasure, hardly knowing how to show their love sufficiently, bidding us welcome with fervent affection, and receiving us as angels of God. Oh, that we may always walk worthy of the vocation wherewith we are called! When I came near the American shore, my very heart melted within me to think from whence I came, where I was going, and what I was going about. But I felt my mind open to the people and my tongue loosed to speak. I feel that God is here and find plenty of all we need.

The following night Frank was invited to speak at St. George's, and as he looked around at the assembled crowd, he realized this was the largest gathering he had ever preached to. He fastened his eyes on the crowd and preached his heart out.

For the next week Frank remained in Philadelphia, praying with people, meeting with Joseph Pilmore, and attending services. On November 6, 1771, he climbed aboard a stagecoach bound for New York City. It was time to present himself to Richard Boardman and find out where his preaching circuits would take him. Since Richard Wright felt he should stay a little longer in Philadelphia and await his orders there, Frank traveled alone.

The trip to New York was unlike anything Frank had ever experienced. The scenery was magnificent. It was late fall. Blazing forests of maple, ash, and red oak trees stretched out to the left as the road followed the twists and turns of the Delaware River to the right. Frank was traveling aboard a brand-new stagecoach service called the Flying Machine, and fly it did. The new service reduced the time needed to cover the ninety miles between Philadelphia and New York from five days to two.

The ride was exhilarating. The stagecoach traveled so fast that it was in constant danger of tipping over. When the coach wheels got in a rut or ran over a tree root, the driver would yell, "Bear to the left" or "Bear to the right," and all the passengers would lean as far as they could in one direction or the other to balance the weight. Frank was glad to break his journey in Burlington, New Jersey, where he spent the night with some local Methodists who had formed a society following Captain Webb's visits to their town.

Frank preached on the courthouse steps that night, and the next morning he climbed back aboard the Flying Machine to travel through Amboy and across Staten Island before catching a ferryboat to New York City on the island of Manhattan. Some new passengers joined the stagecoach for the next leg of the journey, including a serious-looking middle-aged man, who introduced himself as Peter Van Pelt. Frank was about to introduce himself in return but soon discovered he had no need to do so.

"You are just arrived from England, Mr. Asbury. I had the good fortune to hear you preach in Philadelphia at St. George's last week," Peter said.

The two men fell into an awkward conversation as the Flying Machine bumped along. Peter soon invited Frank to spend the night at his house on Staten Island. "I have a house in the village of Woodrow. A small group of Christians live in the village, and I would be honored if you would preach your first sermon in New York in my house."

Since Richard Boardman was not expecting him on any particular day, Frank accepted Peter's invitation. He stayed at the Van Pelt home in Woodrow for several days, preaching there and at the house of the local magistrate, Justice Hezekiah Wright. He was glad for the opportunity to speak to the local Christians, but he wondered whether he was worthy to take on the solemn responsibility of preaching in the colonies. He confided in his journal, "My heart and mouth are open; only I am still aware of my deep insufficiency, and that mostly with regard to holiness. It is true, God has given me some gifts, but what are they compared to holiness? It is for holiness my spirit mourns. I want to walk constantly before God without reproof."

On Monday, November 11, Frank set out for New York City. It was time to meet Richard Boardman. The weather was brisk, and Frank was thankful for the warm set of clothes the Methodists of Bristol had outfitted him with before he left England. He made his way to Stapleton on the northern end of Staten Island and there caught a ferry that took him to Whitehall on the southern tip of Manhattan Island.

While Philadelphia was neatly laid out according to a grid system, with broad clean streets, New York City was the exact opposite. As far as Frank could see, there was no rhyme or reason to the way the streets ran at all sorts of different angles to each other. New York streets were also narrow, muddy, and crowded, and it wasn't uncommon to see pigs and cows roaming freely. Judging by the number of hawkers with horse-drawn carts in the streets selling water, Frank decided the city probably had no adequate supply of fresh drinking water.

Frank wound his way through the narrow city streets and before long was knocking on the door of Richard Boardman's house. The door opened, and Frank introduced himself before being invited in. He was shocked to discover how old and worn the thirty-three-year-old preacher looked. "I've been quite sick lately," Richard explained. "I've done my best since I've been here, with God's help, but being in charge of the New York Society and visiting as many of the others as I can has been quite a burden. I preach at the Wesley Chapel on John Street twice on Sundays and on Tuesday and Thursday nights and hold a society meeting on Wednesday nights. I don't know if I'll ever get down to the Methodists in Frederick, Maryland, with Robert Strawbridge. I think he has three or four chapels and rides the circuit, but I've scarcely been able to put my attention to what they are doing. Strawbridge is a man with a strong faith and fire and has a loyal following."

Frank told Richard how he had enjoyed the missionary letters he had sent back to England and how they played a part in challenging him to come to the American colonies to help strengthen the Methodist work. Now here he was in the colonies talking face-to-face with Richard. Frank also presented Brother Boardman with the twenty pounds and the books the Methodists in Bristol had sent to their brethren in New York. Richard appeared touched by the gesture.

"Now, tell me more about Wesley Chapel here," Frank said. "How long has it been functioning?"

Richard smiled. "Ah, there's a story worth telling!" he said. "The Lord's hand has been on it from the start. As you are probably aware, John Wesley had a particular love for the Irish and rode the circuit in Ireland. Philip Embury was one of his many converts. Once he'd heard the gospel, Philip took to preaching himself, and he became a registered Methodist preacher. Then in 1760, he and a group of relatives left Ireland for New York. I don't know if he was daunted by the task of preaching in a foreign land or overwhelmed by making a living in a new place, but he became a backslider and fell away from his fervent love of the Lord.

"A second group of immigrants arrived a year later, among them his cousin, Barbara Heck. She too had been converted under John Wesley, and no doubt she expected to find that Philip had set up a Methodist Society in New York. He had not. One day, soon after her arrival, she watched some of the 'Methodist men' playing cards. She could take it no longer. She got up, threw the cards in the fireplace, and said, 'Brother Embury, you must preach to us, or we shall all go to hell, and God will require our blood at your hands!' Poor Embury—to him it was like a thunder peal in a clear sky, like the sound of the last trumpet! Her manner, the tone of her voice, and what she said alarmed him."

Frank nodded as he imagined the scene.

Richard continued the story: "'How can I preach, for I have neither a house nor a congregation?' Embury countered. Barbara had an answer for that. 'Preach in your own house and to your own company then.' To God's credit, Philip took up preaching again. Only six attended the first meeting. But their numbers gradually increased until they had to rent a rigging loft on William Street. Then in 1768, Philip and some members of his class donated the money to buy a lot on John Street and started building the church. Philip did a lot of the work himself, including making the pulpit."

"Will I meet him tonight?" Frank asked.

Shaking his head, Richard replied, "No. When I arrived in New York, he had moved to Albany, north of here, to take up a contract manufacturing linen. He's hired a lot of Irish immigrants and preaches every Sunday. The work there is flourishing, though I miss Brother Embury's fellowship. I am fortunate here to have the support of such an able preacher as Captain Webb. But you must visit Albany sometime and see the work of Philip Embury for yourself."

"I would like to do that," Frank agreed. "Perhaps his meetings will become part of my circuit."

Richard shook his head. "I'm not sure you'll be venturing far on a regular basis. There's plenty for you and Richard Wright to do here and in Philadelphia. Since I haven't been in good health, I am looking forward to handing off some of my responsibilities to you."

Frank's heart sank. There were already two Methodist preachers in New York City, and Frank was sure they didn't need a third—not when so much of the rest of the colonies remained untouched by the Methodist message.

That night Frank took his place in the pulpit at Wesley Chapel, a large square building with a pitched roof, located on John Street. As he looked out on the crowd gathered for the meeting, he was surprised to note the fine clothing some of the men and women wore. It would have seemed quite out of place at the Methodist meetinghouse in Bristol, or at any other English Methodist gathering, for that matter.

As the text for his sermon, Frank chose 1 Corinthians 2:2: "For I determined not to know any thing among you, save Jesus Christ, and him crucified."

After he had finished preaching, Frank was introduced to those attending the meeting. He recognized Captain Webb immediately by his eye patch. After talking with him for a few minutes, there was no doubt in Frank's mind that Captain Webb was the larger-than-life figure everyone painted him to be.

Frank's next conversation was with the sexton (caretaker) of the chapel, a black man named Peter Williams who was a slave owned by a tobacconist. The other black person in attendance was a woman named Betty, who was also a slave and a founding member of the chapel.

As Frank walked to his lodging that night, he was deep in thought. So many things in the colonies were different from how they were in England. The whole notion of Christian slaves and owners disturbed him deeply, as did the fine clothes and high manners of some of the New York Methodists. Frank wondered how he would fit into all of this. He could not see himself remaining silent about the evils of slavery, nor could he see himself settling into a position at Wesley Chapel. He had to face the truth: he longed to be on horseback, riding out into the countryside to preach to the poor and the needy. How, he wondered, was that going to happen in the New World when Richard Boardman's plan was to keep the new preachers in Philadelphia and New York rather than letting them follow John Wesley's circuit-riding pattern?

Chapter 6

Dissatisfied

I assume you will stay and help lead the flock in Manhattan," Richard Boardman told Frank. "Everyone seems to like your preaching, and in a few months you can trade places with Richard Wright and preach in Philadelphia."

Frank found what he was hearing hard to believe. In the two weeks he had been in New York he'd preached numerous times at Wesley Chapel. It was good work but not the kind of work a Methodist preacher should be doing—getting comfortable, living in a house, preaching to the same people week in and week out. As far as Frank was concerned, it was a waste of resources.

Even though Captain Webb and his wife had just left to return to England for a while, two registered

Methodist preachers were still working with the same group on an island with a population of eighteen thousand. Frank could not fathom this when over two million others in the thirteen American colonies had no one to preach to them. No, Frank told himself, Brother Boardman has become soft and comfortable in the city. Frank, on the other hand, was eager to get back in the saddle and ride a circuit. John Wesley had sent him here to shine God's light on all the colonies, and Frank was going to find a way to do just that.

This put Frank in a difficult situation. He knew he could not follow Richard Boardman's direction. Even if he was representing John Wesley in the colonies, Richard was not doing things Wesley's way; Frank was sure of that. He weighed his options and decided to write to John about the situation. He also wrote a letter to his parents, telling them all about life in the American colonies and his adventures so far. It would take months for Frank to receive a response to his letter from John Wesley. In the meantime he wondered whether he should go ahead and create his own circuit to ride.

One November morning Frank looked out the window to discover that winter had come early. The houses were covered with snow, and the puddles in the muddy streets had turned to ice. Frank opened his journal and wrote, "At present I am dissatisfied. I judge we are to be shut up in the cities this winter. My brethren seem unwilling to leave the cities, but I think I shall show them the way. I am in trouble, and more trouble is at hand."

With these words, Frank had made up his mind. He was not going to be shut up in New York for the winter. Time was short. Thousands of colonists in the hinterlands around New York City needed to be organized into Methodist Societies, and he was going to lead the way.

Frank set out by stagecoach. He did not own a horse and had convinced two men from Wesley Chapel to accompany him. Their journey took them along the Boston Post Road up the island of Manhattan. Beyond the edge of the city, most of the island was dotted with farms. At the northern end of Manhattan Island, they crossed Kingsbridge over Spuyten Duyvil Creek and onto the mainland. Wherever he went, Frank preached—in houses, jails, and taverns. Sometimes he was well received; other times he was told not to come back.

In January 1772 Frank's two traveling companions had to return to New York, and Frank continued on alone. As he traveled, he stayed with Christian families along the way. He was grateful that his hosts would often ferry him to the next town or village in their wagon or sleigh or would loan him a horse so he could ride. He traveled throughout the settlements of southern New York, preaching and teaching to anyone who would listen.

As he traveled, a harsh winter settled over the land. While England was cold and damp during winter, the combination of snow, ice, and wind in America chilled Frank to his core. Even the warm woolen clothes the Methodists in Bristol had given him seemed inadequate in the face of the biting cold. By the time Frank reached the town of New Rochelle, the cold was taking a toll on his body. His throat felt as if it were on fire, and the pressure in his ears and nose made his head pulsate. Despite feeling miserable, Frank managed to preach several times in New Rochelle before he became so sick he could go on no farther. He took to bed, and his host, Anthony Barrow, called the doctor to come. After examining Frank, the doctor worried that he might choke and die because his throat was so swollen. He administered several medicines, but it was more than a week before Frank could eat again.

More than two weeks passed before Frank was able to get back on the road. This time he headed back down the Boston Post Road to New York. By now Richard Boardman and Joseph Pilmore had switched pastoral positions at their respective churches, and Brother Pilmore was glad to welcome Frank back to the city. But Frank did not stay long. Now that he'd had a taste of preaching in the small towns and villages, he was eager to be on his way. Several of the New York Methodists were touched by his earnestness and his determination to reach out to others with the gospel and took up an offering to buy him a horse and saddle. Frank was delighted by their kindness and generosity and by the dark brown horse and new leather saddle they presented to him. Now he could really get on with the business of being a circuit rider.

In April 1772 the four Methodist preachers— Frank, Richard Wright, Richard Boardman, and Joseph

Pilmore—met in Philadelphia to agree upon where they should all serve for the next few months. Frank worked hard to convince the other men to get out into the countryside to preach in the scattered communities throughout the colonies. Eventually they all decided that Joseph should make a preaching tour south while Richard Boardman went north. Richard Wright would go to New York, and Frank would stay in Philadelphia.

This outcome suited Frank. Now that he had a district of his own, he could set to work. He had two goals. The first was to establish a preaching circuit that would stretch from the head of Chesapeake Bay in the south to Trenton, New Jersey, in the north, a distance of about eighty miles. Frank's second goal was to tighten discipline at St. George's so that members would be in line with John Wesley's Methodist teaching.

Neither job proved easy. At St. George's, Frank started by enforcing the rules on who could attend the closed meetings of the Methodist Society. These meetings were supposed to be a place where committed believers could express themselves, their struggles and problems, and their personal victories and prayer requests. The leader was expected to meet with each participant every three months to ensure that attendees were still following Wesley's rules of prayer, Bible reading, witnessing, and giving to the society. Any society member who had fallen away from doing these things would not get their ticket to attend the private meetings renewed. Over time this practice had been abandoned at St. George's, and anyone was welcome to attend society meetings. This greatly bothered Frank, who believed that Methodists needed someplace where they could privately encourage each other and bear each other's burdens.

On April 25, 1772, Frank stood at the door of St. George's and personally quizzed each person before allowing the person to enter the closed meeting. He turned away many people who were "good" Methodists but admitted that they did not follow Wesley's rules. This was not a popular move. Frank's stand infuriated many people in the congregation, and they started grumbling and complaining about their new preacher. In response Frank wrote, "I heard that many were offended at my shutting them out of the Society meeting, as they had been greatly indulged before. But this does not trouble me. While I stay, the rules must be attended to, and I cannot suffer myself to be guided by half-hearted Methodists."

As word got around, the number of people attending St. George's began to dwindle. Despite this, Frank did not change his views. He had been sent out by John Wesley to follow the pattern laid down by the English Methodists, and he was certain that following that pattern was the right and only way for Methodists to live.

Frank was also certain that the only way for the society to grow in the American colonies was to encourage Methodists to preach the gospel. Accordingly, he began organizing the individuals left in the Methodist Society in Philadelphia to fan out across the colony. He envisioned seven preachers spreading out from the upper reaches of Chesapeake Bay to Trenton.

In the three months that he worked among the Methodists in Philadelphia, Frank managed to fire up those left in the society with a passion for living a holy life and a vision to reach beyond the city. But now it was time for the four Methodist preachers to switch pastoral positions. Frank was to go to New York again, only this time he would be in sole charge of Wesley Chapel.

Throughout this time Frank kept his ears open for any new developments in the growing tension between the British government and the various colonies. While Frank didn't like to talk much about politics, he was concerned about the growing strife between the two groups. In late June, just as he was riding back to New York, Frank heard about the looting and burning of His Majesty's Ship *Gaspée* that had occurred off Rhode Island earlier in the month. The HMS *Gaspée* was sent by the British to patrol the waters around the colony of Rhode Island, looking for ships smuggling goods into the colonies without paying the correct taxes on them. The *Gaspée*'s captain, Lieutenant William Dudingston, often harassed colonial ships without good reason.

On June 9, 1772, while pursuing a ship into Narragansett Bay, the HMS *Gaspée* ran aground. Enraged by the tactics of the *Gaspée*'s captain and crew, the merchants and traders of Rhode Island decided to take advantage of the situation. That night, sixty-seven colonists rowed out to the ship and boarded it. The crew tried to resist, but it was a meager effort during which the captain was shot and wounded. The colonists dragged the crew from their vessel and proceeded to loot the ship before setting it on fire. The HMS *Gaspée* burned to the waterline and was totally destroyed.

When Frank learned of the incident, he sensed that the situation in the colonies would eventually boil over into open fighting. He also knew that this would put the Methodists in a difficult situation, since as a society they were aligned with the Church of England and were therefore seen as loyal to the British. Other churches did not have the same problem. In fact, John Allen, a Baptist minister from Boston, had preached a sermon against the British called "An Oration, Upon the Beauties of Liberty, Or the Essential Rights of the Americans." The text of the sermon had been printed up and was now being widely distributed throughout the colonies. After reading the sermon text, Frank felt more certain that a larger confrontation would develop between the British and the American colonists.

The certainty of eventual conflict in the colonies drove Frank to pray more and work harder at preaching and setting up Methodist Societies around the countryside. Frank believed that every person had eternal value, and some people might well be called up to fight and die sooner than they imagined. They needed to find peace in their souls before that happened.

News and letters from England confused and frustrated Frank. It was obvious to him that no one back there had a good grasp of what was really happening in the American colonies. In August he received a letter from Alexander Mather, a Methodist leader in England, suggesting that all Methodist preachers return to England. Frank was still praying about Mather's suggestion when another letter arrived on October 10, 1772. This letter was from John Wesley himself, and it answered in a surprising way the questions Frank had raised regarding following the Methodist rules. The letter announced that Richard Boardman was to step down from leading the Methodist work in the American colonies and that Frank should take his place.

This was not the answer Frank had been expecting, and he had a mixed reaction to it. On one hand he totally believed in the Methodist plan and was glad to be able to help ensure that it was followed properly. On the other hand, Frank knew that he had made enemies as well as friends during his first year in the colonies, and those enemies could make things very difficult for him. He was, after all, the youngest of the Methodist preachers and the least educated. As he read John's letter one more time, he wondered why people would even want to follow him as their leader. Yet John had chosen him and made him the Methodist leader in the American colonies.

One of the first issues Frank needed to deal with was the matter of Robert Strawbridge. In October Frank had ridden with Robert on a preaching tour around parts of Maryland. The two men got along well, and Frank admired the way Robert had developed many small rural preaching centers instead of trying to raise up city congregations. Robert had the kind of fire a Methodist preacher needed, and the numbers of his converts backed it up.

As a result of Robert's efforts, there were 500 Methodists in Maryland, compared to 180 in both New York and Philadelphia, 200 in New Jersey, and 100 in Virginia. There was just one problem—Robert baptized babies and served communion. According to John Wesley, only ordained ministers in the Church of England should do such things. Methodist preachers were only allowed to preach. Yet the situation in Maryland was not a simple matter. There the Church of England was not the official church. In fact, there were few Anglican churches in the colony. This created a problem for the newly converted Methodists. Where were they supposed to go to get baptized or take communion? Frank did not have an answer, but he could not imagine allowing Robert to carry on doing what he was doing. His actions would alter the way Methodist preachers operated. In the end, Frank and Robert came to a compromise. Frank would write to John for a ruling on the matter. In the meantime, Robert could keep on giving communion and taking on the other roles of an ordained minister.

The answer to Frank's query arrived from John in a form neither Frank nor Robert expected. In Philadelphia in late April 1773, four Methodist men, along with returning Captain Thomas Webb, stepped off a ship just arrived from England: Thomas Rankin, a stern, thirty-five-year-old Scotsman; George Shadford, a thirty-four-year-old athletic Englishman and a trusted friend of Frank's; and two other Englishmen, Joseph Yearbry and Abraham Whitworth.

When the men finally met Frank, Thomas handed him a letter from John Wesley in which John introduced Thomas as his new representative in the American colonies. In one fell swoop, Francis Asbury was swept aside and Captain Webb was appointed over him. Frank was glad to be free of all the administrative responsibilities, but he shuddered to think of the American Methodist movement in the hands of someone who knew nothing about the looming trouble in the colonies.

Chapter 7

A Deepening Crisis

It was July 14, 1773, and Francis Asbury and the other Methodist leaders in the American colonies were attending a General Conference at St. George's in Philadelphia. It was a particularly hot day, and Frank soon tired of all the wrangling and debating going on. But not Thomas Rankin. As the day wore on, Thomas was blunt and tireless in defending his position. He seemed to relish pointing out all the things he thought the Methodists in the colonies were doing wrong. According to Thomas, money had been wasted, poorly suited leaders had been appointed, and far too many rules had been broken. Thomas declared that it was time for Methodists in the colonies to take the rules of the movement more seriously.

Of course, Frank was all for this. He had been trying to get his fellow Methodist preachers to do as much and enforce Methodist rules and discipline. But as he listened to Thomas, he felt uneasy about the tone of the speech. Yes, more attention needed to be paid to enforcing the rules, and yes, better leaders were needed. But as Frank had already discovered, enforcement of some of these things involved unique challenges in the colonies—challenges Thomas, having just arrived from England, did not seem to grasp. *Perhaps he will achieve his goal,* Frank thought, *or perhaps he won't. Only time will tell.*

As the conference in Philadelphia drew to a close, Thomas appointed the Methodist preachers to their new positions. He assigned himself to New York; George Shadford to Philadelphia; and Frank, Robert Strawbridge, Abraham Whitworth, and Joseph Yearbry to the Baltimore area. This decision made Frank happy. He needed time away from Richard Boardman and Joseph Pilmore, as well as from Thomas Rankin, to think things through and experiment with his own kind of circuit riding.

Frank was glad to be headed south to Maryland. So much needed to be done to bring the gospel and Methodist teaching to the outlying communities. Frank was soon busy riding through the countryside. Whenever he stopped to eat or spend the night, he gathered any and all who wanted to listen and preached to them. As he rode his circuit, he often stayed with Methodist or Quaker families, encouraging them in their faith and challenging the young men to take up itinerant preaching, as he had done. When several young men stepped forward to take up the challenge, Frank took them under his wing, rode with them, helped them to understand the Bible, and taught them how to preach. It was just the kind of work he loved the most, but it came to a complete halt in late September 1773.

On Friday, October 1, Frank wrote in his journal:

> I was exceedingly ill at Mr. Dallam's and now began to think my traveling would be interrupted. This is my greatest trouble and pain, to forsake the work of God and to neglect the people, whose spiritual interest and salvation I seek with my whole soul. The next day, finding myself too weak to travel, I . . . content[ed] myself to abide here awhile, where they treat me with the greatest care and kindness. My present purpose is, if the Lord spares and raises me up, to be more watchful and circumspect in all my ways. O Lord, remember me in mercy, and brace up my feeble soul!

Thankfully, at the time he took sick, Frank was staying in northern Maryland with Josiah and Sarah Dallam, a devoted Methodist couple. As Frank's temperature rose dramatically, his hosts recognized his symptoms. Frank had contracted malaria, a common disease in the low-lying areas around Chesapeake Bay. He became delirious, and Sarah attended to him day and night, sponging him with water to cool him down and spooning broth into his mouth.

Frank was so sick that he did not make an entry in his journal for five days—after the initial wave of malaria had passed. On Wednesday, October 6, he wrote, "My . . . body was in great pain for many hours." However, more waves of malaria swept over Frank, leaving him delirious and semiconscious for days. On October 25 he confided in his journal, "My friends wept around and expected my dissolution [death] was near. But the Lord thought on both them and me, to raise me up from the borders of death. Oh that my few remaining days may be spent to His glory!" Frank did not die, and slowly he began to heal, though successive waves of fever surged through his body, keeping him flat on his back in bed.

Frank was still lying in bed recovering at the end of November when he heard the news that seven British East India Company ships had arrived in the colonies. One ship each docked in New York, Philadelphia, and Charleston; three ships docked in Boston; and a fourth ship was due to arrive there any day. The holds of the vessels were filled with boxes of tea from India that were to be unloaded and sold in each of the cities, with a three-penny-per-pound tax added to the price. The Sons of Liberty, a political group made up of American patriots, stirred up the colonists to challenge the tea tax. They pointed out that the colonists were being unfairly taxed by Great Britain, while the British government did not allow them to vote on the things that affected them.

Frank hated to discuss politics. He felt that was best left to others. His calling was to reach and disciple as many new Christians as possible. However, as he lay in bed shivering and sweating from the effects of the malaria, he was sure the matter of the tea tax would not be resolved peacefully. By now a number of American colonists were boiling with rage against Great Britain, and nothing seemed to calm them.

While waves of malaria continued, their intensity began to wane, and Frank soon felt well enough to preach, write in his journal, and mount his horse. It was time to get back to his circuit riding. On December 18, though still feverish, he rode twenty miles through the rain back to Baltimore. When Frank arrived in Baltimore, excitement and dread filled the air. A runner had arrived from Boston and brought news of the actions of the Sons of Liberty. In New York, Philadelphia, and Charleston, colonists had managed to persuade tea merchants not to buy any of the tea the British East India Company ships had brought. Eventually the ship captains had been convinced to return to England with their cargoes of tea.

In Boston things had not gone so easily. Thomas Hutchinson was determined to hold his ground against the colonists and refused to let the ships leave port with their cargoes of tea still aboard. It appeared to be a stalemate. The Sons of Liberty stood guard over the ships, refusing to let them be unloaded. On December 16, 1773, about seven thousand people had gathered at the Old South Meetinghouse in Boston to force the issue. But they could not get Governor Hutchinson to change his mind and agree to send the ships back to England with their cargoes of tea.

Then about one hundred men dressed as Mohawk warriors boarded the three vessels tied up in Boston Harbor and dumped their cargo, 342 chests of tea, into the water.

Frank had a fateful feeling about the outcome of the actions in Boston, but as always, he chose to focus on the spiritual rather than the political. He urged those around him to put their faith in God and work hard to spread the gospel throughout the colonies. He intended to lead by example.

In May 1774, still feeling weak from malaria, Frank made his way to Philadelphia for the second annual Methodist Conference. The many reports given at the conference made him feel stronger. There were now 2,073 Methodists in the American colonies, nearly a thousand more than the year before. And there were seventeen full-time circuit riders instead of ten. Although Frank did not particularly like Thomas Rankin's personal style, he had to admit that under his leadership, Methodism in America was growing.

Frank was not so happy, however, with Thomas's decision to send Richard Boardman and Joseph Pilmore back to England. The two men had left in January and so were not at the meeting. Although he'd had his issues with Richard, Frank hated to see a good preacher leave the colonies, and he wondered if Thomas should have tried harder to win the men over rather than send them home. But Frank did not object when Thomas announced that he was also sending Richard Wright back to England. Although Frank felt sympathy for the man who had accompanied him out to the colonies nearly three years before, he realized that Richard had lost his religious zeal and no longer wanted to preach or talk about Christian matters.

At the conference, Frank asked to be sent back to Baltimore so that he could continue riding the circuit he had established around Maryland, but Thomas insisted he go instead to New York City for the summer quarter. Frank did as he was instructed, though it was not easy. He had heard rumors that Thomas was talking about him behind his back, and a couple of nasty, unsigned letters were circulated regarding Frank that only Thomas had the knowledge to write. On top of this, Frank still suffered from bouts of malaria. In July he calculated that he'd been sick for ten months, but he had still managed to ride nearly two thousand miles and preach three hundred times during that period.

In fact, the Methodists in New York were so alarmed by Frank's poor health that they begged Thomas to allow him to stay with them through two quarters so that they could help look after him. Thomas agreed. Despite his weakened health, Frank continued to preach regularly at Wesley Chapel on John Street. He also headed out to ride a circuit around the rural communities to the north of Manhattan Island.

While Frank was in New York, news arrived in the colonies of the British government's response to the tea incident in Boston Harbor. The British Parliament passed a series of acts that were quickly dubbed the "Intolerable Acts" in the American colonies. One of the acts closed Boston Harbor until the East India Company had been fully reimbursed for the destroyed tea. Another act, the Massachusetts Government Act, put the government of Massachusetts directly under the control of Parliament and the king, who would appoint the colony's leaders. To try to quash further rebellion, this act limited the number of town meetings in Massachusetts to one a year. Parts of the Intolerable Acts placed burdens on other colonies as well, though Massachusetts bore the brunt of the British government's wrath.

As usual, Frank tried to focus on his ministry and not on politics, but he could not ignore the rising complaints about the British government and its attitude toward the colonies. When he first arrived in the American colonies, Frank had been critical of those who complained about England and murmured against the king, but now he was beginning to see things differently. The Intolerable Acts were aptly named. The acts passed by the British Parliament were harsh and punitive and deeply angered the colonists. Frank wondered how this would help the British in the long run.

With so much dissatisfaction in the colonies, Frank was not surprised to learn that fifty-six members from twelve of the colonies had begun meeting at Carpenters' Hall in Philadelphia on September 5, 1774. The gathering, called a Continental Congress, met to craft a response to the passage of the Intolerable Acts. The members discussed an economic boycott of British trade and petitioned King George III, asking him to redress the grievances of those in the colonies. Frank hoped this would ease the tension between Great Britain and the colonists. He did not want the situation to end in war. He knew such an outcome would mean bloodshed and the destruction of people's property and would probably interrupt his preaching and circuit riding.

Frank continued to preach at Wesley Chapel, ride his circuit around the communities of southern New York, and keep an eye on the developing political situation until November 1774, when two new Methodist missionaries, James Dempster and Martin Rodda, arrived from England. One of the missionaries was assigned to take over the work in New York, freeing up Frank for his next rotation to Philadelphia.

Frank was still serving in Philadelphia when news reached the city of a battle in Massachusetts between the Patriot militia and British soldiers, or Redcoats as they were known. After hearing the news, on April 18, 1775, General Thomas Gage, the British military governor of Massachusetts, sent seven hundred soldiers to destroy a cache of guns and ammunition that the colonists had stored in the town of Concord, about ten miles outside of Boston. The Redcoats also planned to arrest Patriot leaders Samuel Adams and John Hancock, who were hiding in the area. However, the Patriot militia had received advance warning of the British raid and were ready for the approaching troops. When the British soldiers reached the town of Lexington on their way to Concord, seventy-five armed militiamen, or Minutemen as they were called, were waiting for them. Though outnumbered, the Minutemen attacked the British. In the fighting, eight Minutemen were killed and ten were injured.

Following the skirmish in Lexington, the Redcoats moved on to Concord, where they found the residents of the town busily moving arms and ammunition to new hiding places in surrounding hamlets. In fact, by the time the Redcoats arrived, most of the supplies had been moved, and the soldiers were able to capture and destroy only a small portion of guns and ammunition. Because Adams and Hancock were nowhere to be found, the Redcoats left empty-handed to return to Boston. But as they made their way back to Boston, Minutemen, local farmers, and townspeople attacked the British along their route. By the time the British soldiers reached Boston, 73 Redcoats had been killed and another 174 had been wounded, while 49 Patriots were killed and 39 were wounded in the day's fighting.

To Frank, and almost everyone else who heard the news in Philadelphia, the fighting in Lexington and Concord marked a new phase in the tension between the British and the colonists. As news of the battle spread, Frank noted that the colonists were becoming united in their hatred of the British. For his part, Frank redoubled his work as a Methodist preacher. As he rode and preached, he sensed that the hearts of the people were more open than before as they faced the sobering possibility of an all-out war with Great Britain.

In response to the fighting at Lexington and Concord, a second Continental Congress was convened in Philadelphia on May 10, 1775. The purpose of this gathering was to manage the colonial war effort and begin moving the colonies toward independence from Great Britain. With only regional militias to fight any further British military incursions in the colonies, the members of the Continental Congress voted to create a Continental army made up of the militia units around Massachusetts. They appointed George Washington of Virginia to be the commanding general of the army.

The Second Continental Congress was still in session at the end of May when Thomas Rankin dispatched Frank to Norfolk, Virginia, situated at the mouth of Chesapeake Bay, to strengthen the Methodists there. Frank was eager to leave behind the confines of ministry in Philadelphia, and as soon as possible he boarded a boat that took him to Norfolk.

Norfolk and neighboring Portsmouth had a reputation of being a "dry and barren land" spiritually. Frank soon discovered this for himself. The members of the Methodist Society there were undisciplined and obeyed few of the rules that John Wesley had laid down for Methodists to follow. Frank tried to correct this and enforce the rules, but this proved to be much more difficult than it had been in Philadelphia or New York. The local Methodists resisted Frank's efforts, telling him that the society meetings should be open to all who wanted to attend. They also pointed out to Frank that they felt he was too focused on exposing people's faults, and instead of trying to force rules on them, he should be out preaching the gospel. Frank found their attitude troublesome, but he did not back off in his attempt to tighten Methodist discipline on the local society. Despite his best efforts, after a few weeks in Norfolk, the number of people regularly attending Methodist Society meetings was less than half of what it had been when he arrived.

On August 7, 1775, as Frank toiled away in Norfolk, he received a letter from Thomas Rankin. He hesitated to open it because he was sure it would contain some new criticism of his methods. When he finally read the letter, its contents startled him. After reading the letter twice, he wrote down his thoughts in his journal:

> I received a letter from Mr. Thomas Rankin, in which he informed me that [he], Mr. Rodda, and Mr. Dempster had consulted and deliberately concluded it would be best to return to England. But I can by no means agree to leave such a field for gathering souls to Christ as we have in America. It would be an eternal dishonor to the Methodists that we should all leave three thousand souls who desire to commit themselves to our care. Neither is it the part of a good shepherd to leave his flock in time of danger; therefore, I am determined, by the grace of God, not to leave them, let the consequence be what it may.

As Washington toiled to shape the various militias into a single army, Frank heard the reports of more skirmishes between Patriot militias and the Redcoats, but these fights were mostly farther north in the New England area. Slowly, though, the conflict with Great Britain began to engulf the entire coast of North America. Frank encountered this firsthand while riding a circuit to the smaller outlying communities around Norfolk. As Frank rode near Suffolk, two armed militiamen who said they had orders to inspect every passerby stopped him on the road. Since he was English, they questioned him thoroughly as to why he was in the area, where he was going, and what he intended to do when he got there. When they were finally satisfied with his answers, they allowed him to ride on. But the experience left a hollow feeling in the pit of Frank's stomach. Frank knew it was going to get more difficult—possibly even dangerous—for Methodist preachers to travel around their circuits, and more so if they were English.

Despite the danger, Frank was determined not to leave the American colonies and return to England as Thomas and a number of the other English Methodist preachers were planning to do. North America was his mission field, and that was where he would stay.

Chapter 8

Trembling and Shaking

While Frank toiled in and around Norfolk, news reached him of a revival taking place seventy-five miles west in Brunswick County, Virginia. Frank's friend George Shadford, assisted by four other preachers, was overseeing a circuit there. In early November 1775, Frank decided that it was time to head west and visit George.

When he arrived in Brunswick, Frank was delighted to meet up with George again. It felt good to talk with someone about his family and home, someone who did not question Frank's love of England or his loyalty to the colonists. Even more exciting for Frank were George's reports of revival in the area. George explained how large crowds would attend meetings and listen carefully as he preached.

"It's quite common in these meetings for sinners to begin trembling and shaking and fall to the floor under conviction of their sins," George told Frank. "This is only the beginning," he added. "Following these meetings we are careful to get new converts into classes and teach them how to live holy lives. As a result there are many Methodist groups spread throughout the Brunswick circuit."

Frank was impressed with the work his friend was doing. George had built a strong and thriving Methodist community throughout Brunswick County and North Carolina. Frank was even more impressed when he accompanied George to meetings. Not only was George a powerful preacher, but as George had described, under the conviction of sin, people indeed began shaking and trembling and falling to the floor, crying out to God for mercy and forgiveness. Frank was deeply moved by the experience.

Frank was also impressed with the way George had appointed several gifted local men to serve as preachers and oversee the discipling of the new converts. If only all the Methodist circuits in the American colonies had this level of fervency and organization!

While visiting George, Frank had the pleasure of meeting a man who had played a major role in the revival. Devereux Jarratt was a passionate, forty-three-year-old man from Virginia who served as the Church of England minister for Bath Parish in Dinwiddie County. Devereux explained to Frank how, on becoming the leader of the Bath Parish, he had decided to preach only the evangelical doctrines found in the New Testament. He preached these doctrines with such zeal and conviction that many parish members fell under conviction of their sins as they listened to him speak.

Devereux had gone to Great Britain to train as a minister in the Church of England. While there he had his first contact with Methodists, hearing both John Wesley and George Whitefield preach. He was impressed by both men and by the Methodist Societies as an evangelical movement within the Church of England. When he returned to America and the revival started to spread beyond Bath Parish and Dinwiddie County, Devereux teamed up with the Methodists to organize those being converted into Methodist Societies. The revival seemed to show no signs of slowing down, having spread throughout Virginia and into North Carolina. Indeed, the Methodist Societies in Virginia were now the fastest growing in all of the American colonies.

Frank was still visiting George in December 1775 when the fighting between the colonists and the British moved farther south. On December 9, a battle was fought in the area of Great Bridge, Virginia, just south of Norfolk. The battle ended in a victory for the Patriots that forced Lord Dunmore, the Loyalist governor of Virginia, to flee the colony to British naval ships offshore.

When he received news of the battle, Frank wrote, "We have awful reports of slaughter at Norfolk and the Great Bridge, but I am at a happy distance from them and my soul keeps close to Jesus Christ." In his heart Frank knew the truth. Outright, widespread warfare between Great Britain and the American colonies now seemed unavoidable. Frank wondered how much longer he could remain untouched by the growing conflict.

Frank continued staying with George in Brunswick, where he tried to keep his mind on the revival, saving souls, and the growth of Methodist Societies throughout the area. Yet the struggle between the colonies and Great Britain was never far away. In January 1776, word reached Brunswick County that four British naval ships patrolling off the coast of Virginia had shelled the town of Norfolk on New Year's Day. Over the next two days the entire town burned to the ground. Frank tried not to be alarmed by the news and wrote, "We have constant rumors about the disagreeable war which is now spreading through the country, but all these things I still commit to God."

Frank could not, however, ignore a pamphlet written by John Wesley and titled *A Calm Address to Our American Colonies* that arrived in March from England. Just months before, Wesley had written a letter to the Methodist preachers in America, urging them to stick to the business of preaching, maintain their unity, and remain as neutral as possible. Frank had heartily agreed with this advice and did his best to follow it. But now, as he read John's latest advice, he could scarcely take it in:

> The grand question which is now debated (and with warmth enough on both sides) is this, Has the English Parliament power to tax

the American Colonies? . . . Nothing can be more plain, that the supreme power of England has a legal right of laying any tax upon them for any end beneficial to the whole empire. . . . In wide-extended dominions, a very small part of the people are concerned with making laws. This, as all public business, must be done by delegation; the delegated are chosen by a select number. And those who are not electors, who are far the greater part, stand by, idle and helpless spectators. . . . You are descendants of men who either had no votes or resigned them by emigration. You have therefore exactly what your ancestors left you: not a vote in making laws nor in choosing legislators, but the happiness of being protected by laws and the duty of obeying them.

Frank was shocked by these words. He wondered what had happened. Instead of remaining neutral, John Wesley had come out firmly in favor of the British and was telling the American colonists that they must submit to England.

John's pamphlet, which was supposed to calm down the rebellion against Great Britain, had the opposite effect. Although Frank concluded that John meant well in writing it, in doing so John had stirred up a lot of suspicion and hatred toward the Methodists. Frank would have to wait and see what would happen next.

Frank stayed in Brunswick County, Virginia, until early March 1776, when he left to return to

Philadelphia. Along the way he visited Methodist Societies where he preached and encouraged the locals in their faith. He also spent time in Baltimore, where he found many residents of the city deeply alarmed by the news that British naval ships were patrolling off the coast of Maryland. Residents worried that the ships might enter Chesapeake Bay and attack the city.

In Baltimore, Frank was surprised to find Martin Rodda. From the letter he had received from Thomas Rankin seven months before, Frank assumed that Thomas, Martin, and James Dempster had all returned to England by now. Instead he learned that Thomas and Martin had changed their minds and were both still serving in the American colonies.

After spending time in Baltimore, Frank moved on and spent the months of April and May traveling around Pennsylvania and New Jersey, preaching and visiting Methodist Societies. Then, on May 27, he received word that Thomas had appointed him to Baltimore to oversee the work there.

Frank was glad to be heading to Maryland again. He had spent much time there in the past and established several circuits, and he looked forward to going back and renewing acquaintances, preaching the gospel, and strengthening Methodists throughout the area, especially given the uncertainty of the times.

Less than a month after arriving in Baltimore, Frank fell sick again. This time it was not malaria but a severely ulcerated throat. While he recuperated, he stayed with Henry and Prudence Gough. Henry was a successful and wealthy merchant in Baltimore, who along with his wife had joined the Methodists as a result of Frank's previous round of preaching there. The Goughs owned an eleven-hundred-acre estate called Perry Hall, located to the northeast of Baltimore. The Goughs' home was the most magnificent house Frank had ever stayed in. It reminded him of Hamstead Hall, where his father had been employed as a gardener back in England. Frank was much more at home in humble dwellings, and at first he found it difficult to relax at the estate.

While staying with the Goughs, Frank heard news that in Philadelphia on July 4, 1776, a document called a Declaration of Independence had been presented to the Continental Congress. The document contained a formal explanation as to why the members of the Continental Congress had voted two days before to declare independence from Great Britain. The thirteen American colonies now regarded themselves as independent states and were no longer a part of the British Empire.

When he heard the news, Frank was not surprised that the colonies had taken this step. As he saw it, the grievances between the colonies and Great Britain had created a divide too great for repair. The American colonies were now fighting a war for independence. Frank was glad that such a man of godly character as George Washington was leading the fight for the colonies.

Frank's recovery was slow. His ulcerated throat and the lingering effects of malaria had taken a toll.

He was only thirty-one years old, but he felt as if he were eighty. The Goughs insisted on paying for Frank to go to Berkeley Springs in northwestern Virginia to relax and recuperate. It was a place where the well-to-do came to relax, socialize, and bathe in the mineral springs. Henry accompanied Frank across Maryland to the springs and helped him settle in. Like Perry Hall, Berkeley Springs reminded Frank that he came from humble roots.

For a man who was used to accounting for how he spent every minute of every day, Frank found it impossible to simply relax. He did the only thing he knew how to do—he set about making good use of his time. While he soaked in the mineral springs, he read biographies of inspiring people, making it his goal to read at least one hundred pages a day. He prayed five times a day in public, preached in the open air every other day, and held public prayer meetings each evening, where he would also give lectures on spiritual matters.

With a routine now in place, Frank felt much happier, though he did notice that some people tended to avoid him. Nonetheless, he stayed six weeks at Berkeley Springs recuperating before heading back to Baltimore. When he left Berkeley Springs, he noted, "I this day turned my back on the springs, as the best and worst place that I ever was in—good for health but most injurious to religion." Frank resumed his duties in Baltimore, overseeing the Methodist work in the city and developing a circuit around Annapolis.

Shortly after his return to Baltimore, Frank learned that Washington and his ragtag Continental army had been defeated in the Battle of Long Island. He was glad to learn that Washington's troops had made a daring escape in the middle of the night to avoid capture by the British. Soon afterward, the British took control of Manhattan Island and the city of New York.

In the weeks that followed, the Continental army suffered a number of defeats at the hands of the British, raising the anxiety level of the American colonists. As he traveled around preaching, Frank was well aware of how fearful people were about the outcome of the war. Always he tried to focus people's attention back on spiritual matters. He hoped the Americans would win, but he left the outcome to God and encouraged others to do the same.

In late December 1776, Frank heard news that made his stomach churn. This time it concerned Thomas Rankin and Captain Webb. The two were both strong Loyalists and supporters of King George III, and Webb had gone so far as to spy for the British. Webb was assigned to the Methodist circuit in New Jersey, and he had secretly crossed the Delaware River into Pennsylvania. There he learned that Washington was planning a daring attack at Christmas on the British troops wintering over at Trenton, New Jersey. Captain Webb rushed back to his home in New Jersey, where Thomas was staying with him, and told what he had learned about the secret attack.

Together Webb and Thomas had gone to the British commander and reported the plans. Fortunately for the colonists, the British did not believe Webb's story. Unfortunately for the British, Washington's troops did secretly cross the Delaware River on the night of December 25 and attack the unsuspecting British troops on the morning of December 26. The battle was a resounding victory for Washington and the Continental army. Following the battle, when they learned of Webb's treachery, militiamen in New Jersey tracked Webb down and expelled him from the colony. Thomas managed to avoid arrest and headed for Pennsylvania.

When Frank heard what the two Methodist leaders had done, he was dumbfounded. The Methodists were already under increased suspicion because of their close association with the Church of England. How could they take such a stand and put the life of every Methodist preacher, including his own, in jeopardy?

Throughout 1777, Frank remained in Maryland riding the circuits and preaching, but it was not easy. As an Englishman associated with the Church of England, he had to be constantly vigilant of those who assumed he was a Loyalist.

As the war with the British raged on, the Continental army experienced defeats and victories, sending the emotions of the colonists up and down depending on the latest fighting report. In late September tensions ran high in Maryland as British troops, under the command of General William Howe, captured and occupied Philadelphia. Good news, however, arrived in Baltimore. Continental army forces had defeated British General John Burgoyne's forces at Saratoga in New York, causing Gentleman Johnny, as the general was nicknamed, to surrender his army of nearly seven thousand men to the Americans.

With the British close at hand in Philadelphia, things became even more difficult for Frank. Any Englishman in the area was now a perceived threat. Several incidents did not help Frank's situation. One involved a man who had been associated with the Methodists. Chauncey Clowe had formed a company of about three hundred Loyalists who tried to fight their way through Continental army lines to join the British. Their attempt failed, and Clowe was captured, tried, and executed. Because of Clowe's connection with the Methodists, however, colonists were hardened in their belief that all Methodists, and particularly English Methodist preachers, were British supporters.

In October 1777, Martin Rodda began handing out tracts supporting the British. Members of the Continental army tracked him down, and he barely managed to escape with his life. If a slave had not helped him escape to a British ship, he would surely have been tried and hanged for treason. Thomas Rankin preached one last sermon against the colonial rebels and then slipped behind British lines into Philadelphia, where he spent the winter. Meanwhile, Captain Webb, who had been banished from New Jersey, chose to return there. He was promptly arrested and placed in an internment camp in Bethlehem, Pennsylvania. Two months later, Washington exchanged him for a Patriot prisoner, and Webb was allowed to return to England.

George Shadford, who was still in Virginia, and Frank were the two last English-born Methodist preachers actively preaching in the American colonies. As he contemplated his situation, Frank wrote in his journal, "Three thousand miles from home—my friends have left me—I am considered by some as an enemy of the country—every day liable to be seized by violence, and abused. This is just a trifle to suffer for Christ, and the salvation of souls. Lord, stand by me!"

Frank had come to North America to preach the gospel, and he was determined to continue doing so. He realized, though, that given the present circumstances, this was going to be a challenging task.

Chapter 9

Under Suspicion

By March 1778, reports had filtered back to Baltimore from Valley Forge, Pennsylvania, where Washington's Continental army of twelve thousand soldiers was wintering over. The reports were grim. Apparently twenty-five hundred soldiers had died during the winter from war wounds, disease, and malnutrition. The Continental army was ill equipped to face the harsh winter conditions. Still, Washington and his senior officers were doing all they could to keep morale up. As Frank heard the reports, he wondered how much longer the Patriots could carry on. There were no soft edges to the war now. All glamour had been stripped away, leaving only the harsh realities of hardship and death, victory and defeat.

At the beginning of the rebellion in the American colonies, only about one colonist in three had supported the rebels' cause. By now, many of those who disagreed had left for Canada or the Caribbean Islands, returned to England, or fled westward across the mountains into Indian country. As the war dragged on, the Patriots tried desperately to root out British sympathizers in their midst. In Maryland it became a requirement that every man between the ages of sixteen and sixty prepare himself for military service as well as take an oath to defend the colony and report anyone he believed to be a traitor to the cause.

No man could now preach in the colony without taking the oath. This posed a problem for Frank. Purely on religious grounds he would not take the oath or bear arms. So if he stayed in Maryland, it was only a matter of time before he would be arrested. The decision was obvious to Frank but difficult to make. Despite his desire to keep riding the preaching circuits in Maryland, he needed to find somewhere to lie low for a while.

Frank quietly made his way to the home of Judge Thomas White in Kent County, near Dover, Delaware. Judge White, a devout Methodist with whom Frank had often stayed in the past, offered him refuge. The judge's home was a safe place to be. In Delaware preachers were not required to take an oath of allegiance as they were in Maryland. As an Englishman, however, Frank knew he still had to be very careful.

Shortly after Frank arrived in Delaware, his friend George Shadford visited him at Judge White's home. George brought news that Thomas Rankin had recently left Philadelphia to return to England. Frank and George talked about their predicament as English preachers in North America. Both men loved to teach and preach, but it was becoming harder for them to do so openly. They talked long into the night, but they found few answers to their situation.

"Let's have a day of prayer and fasting for the Lord to direct us. We've never been in such circumstances as Methodist preachers before," George said.

"Let's do so indeed," Frank agreed.

The next day the two men fasted and prayed. Several times Frank walked into the thick woods that surrounded Judge White's house and knelt to pray. In the evening Frank and George got together to discuss what God had shown them.

"And what did the Lord reveal to you regarding our future?" George asked.

"I do not see my way clear to return to England," Frank replied.

"And I cannot stay," George said. "I believe I have done the work here for which I was called, and I feel that I am to return home. I feel this to be the right direction for me now as much as I did when I first felt called to come to these shores."

"Then one of us must be under a delusion," Frank said, his brow furrowed. "Surely God will direct us both the same way."

"Not so," George retorted. "I have a call to go, and you a call to stay. We must obey the call of Providence to each of us."

Frank knew that George was right. God had placed separate calls upon their lives, and Frank's was to remain in America.

The next two days were painful for Frank as he prepared to say goodbye to his closest friend. He had no idea if the two of them would ever see each other again. Frank also realized that when his parents learned that all of the English-born Methodist preachers had returned home from America except him, they would be worried. He wrote a long letter explaining his decision to stay behind. George agreed to deliver the letter.

When the time came to separate, George mounted his horse and rode away from the White estate, leaving Frank to watch him disappear among the trees. Later George wrote of the departure saying, "We saw we must part, though we loved each other as David and Jonathan."

It was a wrenching moment for Frank, who was now the last English Methodist preacher left. As he watched George ride away, Frank felt very alone. Yet he knew he had been called to stay for a reason, and as best he could, given his circumstances, he would focus back on his ministry.

Judge White's nephew, Edward White, lived about a mile away from his uncle. He urged Frank to use his home and barn if he needed to. The large wooden barn proved to be a good place for the Methodists to hold their quarterly meeting. It was cold and drafty, but it was away from prying eyes. Even though no one had been appointed as the leader of the Methodists with the departure of the English preachers, everyone looked to Frank to guide them. After all, he was now the only Methodist preacher in the colonies directly sent out by John Wesley. Frank assumed the role. He preached to the crowd that had gathered for the meeting on the last three verses of Psalm 48: "Walk about Zion, and go round about her: tell the towers thereof. Mark ye well her bulwarks, consider her palaces; that ye may tell it to the generation following. For this God is our God for ever and ever: he will be our guide even unto death."

As he preached, Frank was aware that some of those listening to him could well be killed in the fighting before they had the chance to meet again. Nonetheless, he encouraged the American-born preachers to go about the business of preaching the gospel as boldly and as best they could.

When the conference was over, Frank was left alone with his thoughts. It was difficult for him to watch everyone leave, going off to preach and teach, while he was holed up in a house in Delaware. He poured his thoughts out in his journal: "My temptations were very heavy, and my ideas were greatly contracted in preaching, neither was my soul happy as at many other times. It requires great resignation for a man to be willing to be laid aside as a broken instrument." By the following day Frank had resigned himself to his new life, writing, "I applied myself to the Greek and Latin Testament; but this is not to me like preaching the gospel. However, when a man cannot do what he would, he must do what he can."

One of the men who had been at the conference in the barn was named Freeborn Garrettson. He was an energetic, intelligent twenty-five-year-old who was thoroughly American, being the third generation of his family born in the colonies. The Garrettson family owned land in Hartford County, Maryland, where Freeborn had first encountered Methodist ways when he heard Robert Strawbridge preach. Frank was glad when Freeborn agreed to take over riding the Kent circuit in Delaware. Like Frank, Freeborn had refused to take the oath of allegiance in Maryland, which precluded him from preaching there. Frank hoped that Freeborn, as an American-born preacher, would not be a target for mob violence.

Within days of Freeborn's departure to ride his circuit and preach, news filtered back to Frank that a Queen Anne County judge had confronted Freeborn, knocking him off his horse and beating him senseless with a stick. Freeborn stayed with local Methodists long enough to recover from the beating. As he then rode on, a mob, including a man with a gun, accosted him. Several women riding with Freeborn leaped from their horses and wrestled the gun from the man's hands, allowing Freeborn to escape.

Such news made Frank pray more than ever. The times were challenging for Methodist preachers. With British troops occupying Philadelphia, the suspicion was more palpable than ever, as were efforts to root out Loyalists. No one garnered more suspicion than Francis Asbury did. Frank continued to lie low at the White home.

Within a month of Frank's taking refuge in Delaware, a group of local militiamen barged into the Whites' mansion. Frank stayed out of sight in an upstairs room, though he could hear all that was going on below. The militiamen demanded that Judge White go with them. As Frank covertly looked out the window, he could see the militiamen push his host into a waiting carriage. As soon as they left, Frank hurried downstairs. The judge's wife and several of his children sat weeping, afraid they would never see him again. Frank prayed with them and fasted for the judge's safe return.

After staying three more days at the White home, Frank decided it was too dangerous for the family to shelter him any longer. He packed his saddlebags, bade the family goodbye, and rode off feeling like Abraham, not knowing where he was going or what he would do.

After riding fifteen miles north, Frank stopped at a cabin in the woods. An unusual amount of activity was taking place around it. Frank soon realized that the people who lived there were preparing for a funeral service, but they had no one to lead it. Frank used the opportunity to preach to those gathered about eternal life. Following the funeral, Frank headed off again in a northwesterly direction and crossed into Maryland. That evening a stranger took him in for the night, and the following day Frank moved on. Since there were rumors of Patriot mobs in the area, Frank headed for nearby swampland. He felt like a runaway slave. When he reached the edge of the swampland, he dismounted and waited until far into the night before continuing.

Frank found his way to the home of John Fogwell near Sudlersville, Maryland. John was a dedicated Methodist who had been a drunkard before being converted by the preaching of a blind evangelist named Mrs. Rogers. Frank was grateful when John invited him to stay for a while, even though he knew the risks of doing so. But all went well, and Frank spent the next three weeks praying and studying his Greek New Testament. When Frank finally learned that Judge White had been paroled, he cautiously made his way again to the Whites' estate in Delaware.

Thomas White and his family warmly welcomed Frank back. Judge White explained that he had been arrested on suspicion of being a Tory, or Loyalist supporter, but at his trial he had been cleared of any wrongdoing. Frank was glad his old friend was safe, although upon his return to Delaware he learned that many Methodists had been jailed for preaching in Maryland. One of them, Joseph Hartley, was sentenced to three months in the Talbot County Jail for preaching without a license. Even though he was in prison for preaching, he would not give up. He passionately preached to fellow prisoners and to passersby through his cell window. So many people were converted that the jailer feared Joseph would influence the entire town if he were kept in prison much longer! Although Frank was concerned about Joseph, he smiled as he imagined him preaching his heart out from his jail cell.

Throughout 1778, Frank tried to use his time wisely. He prayed hourly for every preacher on a circuit; studied Greek, Latin, and Hebrew; and read through many of the spiritual books that Judge White and his nephew owned. He also held meetings in Edward White's barn and in neighboring homes. Still, Frank wanted to do more. It was hard for him to be hiding out, unable to travel and preach freely. For a while he even considered leaving America and going to the Caribbean Islands, where he felt he could be useful. But as he prayed, Frank felt he was to stay where he was and do what he could to strengthen his Methodist brothers and sisters. Sometimes, though, he found himself thinking of England and wondering whether George had delivered the letter to his parents.

The war with the British seemed to be at a stalemate, with neither side able to muster enough military resources to deliver the winning punch. However, a couple of bright spots appeared during 1778. First, the Americans entered into a treaty with France, Great Britain's old rival, which would provide French troops to help them fight the British. And in June, the British ended their occupation of Philadelphia, withdrawing their troops and marching overland to New York to strengthen the British forces there. With the British no longer breathing down their necks, people throughout the region relaxed a little.

The year 1778 gave way to 1779, and in March, after staying with the Whites for a year, Frank received some good news. Early on in the rebellion he had written a letter to Thomas Rankin in which

he expressed his thoughts on the war. Frank wrote
to his superior that he believed it would not be long
before the colonies were a free and independent
nation and that he felt too bound to the Americans
to leave them. Unbeknownst to Frank, the letter had
been intercepted by rebel officials and made its way
to the attention of Governor Caesar Rodney of Delaware. When the governor read the letter, he realized
that Francis Asbury was not a British supporter, and
he issued an order allowing Frank to travel freely
within Delaware.

Frank was relieved to know he could travel farther afield within Delaware and be more open in his
actions. One of the first things he did was organize
a conference for northern Methodists (those living north of the Potomac River) to be held at Judge
White's estate on April 28, 1779. He learned that the
southern Methodists in Virginia and North Carolina were planning to hold their own conference.
Frank wished he could attend this conference too,
but although he could now travel within Delaware,
he did not yet feel he could travel freely in other
states.

The outcomes of the two conferences were far-
reaching. The northern conference reaffirmed its
support for the Methodist rules and practices as laid
down by John Wesley and committed to continue
to operate as a religious society. But in the southern
Methodist region, conditions were different. As a
result of the revival in Virginia and North Carolina,
several thousand Methodists now lived throughout

that area. The problem was that as a result of the struggle with Great Britain for independence, most Church of England ministers had returned to England. In fact, the legislature of Virginia had officially removed the Church of England's status as the established church of the state. This meant that few ministers were in the region to administer the sacraments of baptism and communion to the new converts. Confronted with this reality, the Methodist preachers at the southern conference voted to ordain Methodist preachers to do this themselves.

Frank had a heavy heart when he heard the decision of the southern conference. The southern Methodists had chosen a path that would take them in a very different direction from that of their northern brethren.

Throughout 1779, Frank traveled around Delaware. It felt good to him to be once again free to move about. As he traveled, Frank kept an ear out for news of the war, but little seemed to be happening, at least on the battlefield. Then the fighting heated up again in April 1780, when the British attacked and occupied Charleston, South Carolina.

At the time he learned of the British attack on Charleston, Frank was preparing for a special meeting of the northern Methodists to be held in the new Lovely Lane Chapel in Baltimore, Maryland, on April 24, 1780. By now Frank's friends and associates had decided that it was safe for Frank to travel beyond the borders of Delaware, and Frank was eager to be moving.

The main conference for all Methodist preachers—northern and southern—was to be held in Manakin-town near Richmond, Virginia. Frank had called the special meeting in Baltimore to make sure that all of the northern Methodist preachers were agreed that they should not be baptizing people or administering communion to them. The northern Methodists were firm in their resolve, as was recorded in the minutes of the meeting:

> *Question:* Does the whole Conference disapprove the step our brethren have taken in Virginia?
> *Answer:* Yes.
> *Question:* Do we look upon them no longer as Methodists in connection with Mr. Wesley and us till they come back?
> *Answer:* Agreed.
> *Question:* Shall Brothers Asbury, Garrettson, and Watters attend the Virginia Conference and inform them of our proceedings in this and receive their answer?
> *Answer:* Yes.
> *Question:* What must be the conditions of our union with our Virginian brethren?
> *Answer:* To suspend all their administrations for one year, and all meet together in Baltimore.

When the meeting of the northern Methodists was over, Francis Asbury, Freeborn Garrettson, and William Watters left together to ride south to

Manakintown, Virginia. Frank had only one prayer on his lips for the upcoming conference: *God, please help us to stay together as one people. Do not let our divisions tear us apart.*

Chapter 10

A Compromise

On May 9, 1780, Frank stepped into the house of Thomas Smith in Manakintown, Virginia, where the Methodist Conference was about to begin. He felt a chill in the air as he shook hands with the gathered southern preachers. As the day progressed, groups of men met to whisper in corners or stroll in small groups outside. Some failed to look Frank in the eye when he spoke to them, and others told him to his face that they thought he was wrong to side with John Wesley on the baptism and communion issues. It was a difficult two days of conference for Frank, two days he likened to being in a wasp's nest.

Frank knew that if he agreed that the southern preachers could administer communion and baptize people, he would be breaking the bond John expected to exist between Methodist Societies and the Church of England. If the Methodists set themselves up to do these two things, they were, in fact, setting themselves up as a separate denomination. The Methodists would stop being a society and instead become the Methodist Church. That was a monumental step, one Frank found unacceptable. He had come to North America to help establish the Methodist pattern, not reinvent it. If the southern preachers insisted on making their own rules, Frank knew he would have no choice but to cut them off from fellowship and return to England to explain how things had gone so wrong in the colonies. That was a terrible thing to contemplate.

Frank hardly slept during the first night of the conference. He understood the point of view of the southern preachers, even agreeing with them on many points. Yes, because of the war a large number of Church of England ministers had fled back to England and their churches had been closed, leaving many new members of the Methodist Societies with no one authorized to baptize or administer communion to them. Yes, the society members in remote areas appreciated having communion. Yes, some Church of England ministers who hadn't fled were corrupt and unworthy to give communion. Even when confronted with these arguments, Frank remained a close follower of the pattern for the societies laid down by John Wesley, and John did not want Methodist preachers assuming the role of Church of England ministers. At least Frank assumed John still didn't. Given the turmoil in North America, it was difficult to know for sure, and it had been four years since he had received a letter from John.

By the last night of the conference, it was obvious that the southern Methodist preachers were not prepared to give in on the matter of administering the sacraments. They had seen the advantages of acting like a church, and they made it clear they would not go back to society status.

Frank was heartbroken and bitterly disappointed. He did not know how he was going to break the news to John. As soon as he could be alone, Frank sank to his knees and, with tears coursing down his cheeks, poured out his heart to God. He barely slept that night, knowing that the next morning he would have to say goodbye to the southern Methodist preachers—perhaps for the last time. There would be no point in their meeting together after this, since they had decided to go their separate way from the rest of the Methodists in North America.

The next morning as Frank stood on the steps of Thomas Smith's house, where the southern preachers had gathered to eat breakfast, the door swung open.

"Come in, brother," one of the southern preachers said. "We have something interesting to report."

Frank frowned. He had no idea what could have put the preacher at the door in such a good mood when Frank had come to say a gloomy farewell. When he entered the parlor where the southern preachers sat eating breakfast, the men stood and offered him hearty handshakes. The whole scene confused Frank.

One of the southern preachers announced to Frank, "We came to a decision in the night. The decision to break away from fellowship with our northern brethren does not sit well with us, so we have agreed to a compromise."

Frank felt his frown turn into a smile, but he dared not hope for too much.

The preacher went on, "We will stop giving communion and baptizing for one year, long enough to send a letter to John Wesley explaining our side of the story and asking him for permission to change the rules. We also ask that you ride the circuits here in the South so you can see for yourself the predicament we are in."

As Frank stood in the parlor, tears welled up in his eyes. One by one the men embraced him. Frank felt like the father in the parable of the prodigal son when his son came home again. Waves of relief washed over him as he sat down to eat breakfast with the men. Frank could hardly believe how well things had ended. Half of the Methodists in North America were not going to go their own way after all.

Having agreed to ride all the circuits in the South, Frank had to make new plans. But this was not difficult for a man whose only belongings fit into his saddlebags. Later that day Frank left Manakintown, but instead of heading north to Delaware again, he pointed his horse south and headed out to ride the circuits.

Throughout the summer of 1780, Frank rode his horse or traveled by carriage through much of

Virginia and North Carolina. The war for independence continued, and with the British now controlling
Charleston and South Carolina, it was not unusual
for Frank to run into brigades of American and British soldiers. It was also not unusual for soldiers from
both sides to slip into meetings to hear Frank preach.
As he rode, Frank had to be cautious. Horses were
in short supply, and military men from both sides
seized the horses of those they encountered. Thankfully, no one demanded Frank's horse from him. One
night, however, after he had ridden between two
opposing detachments of soldiers, Frank took off his
hat and noticed it had a bullet hole through it. He did
not know which side had fired on him, and he didn't
really care. He was just glad that God had protected
him from harm.

The South, particularly North Carolina, was different from anything Frank had seen before. Many
people lived in rickety houses made of sticks and
mud. There were few schools for the children to
attend, and even fewer churches. Still, Frank found
devout Methodists among them, and he preached
wherever he found people who would listen. Sometimes he preached in tiny log cabins; other times in
large tobacco storehouses where up to five hundred
people would squeeze in to hear him.

As he visited the Methodist circuits in the South,
Frank usually traveled twenty or more miles a day
on rocky, overgrown roads, swimming his horse
across rivers, leading the animal more often than riding because of the terrain, and fending off an endless

number of ticks and chiggers (mites). When there was not enough space on the floor of a cabin for him to bed down at night, Frank would go out into the woods and sleep, using his saddle as a pillow.

The people he met along the way were mostly poor and illiterate, quite different from the folks in New York or Philadelphia. Frank marveled at how low human beings could stoop under such difficult circumstances, noting, "The people are poor and cruel to one another; some families are ready to starve for want of bread, while others have corn and rye distilled into poisonous whiskey; and a Baptist minister has been guilty of the same."

As he rode and walked the southern circuits, Frank had plenty of time to think about another issue he was afraid could tear Methodism apart—slavery. In the South, Frank saw slaves working in the fields cutting corn and tobacco, picking cotton, or chopping wood. In the evenings, some slave owners would bring their slaves to hear Frank preach, while others forbade them to attend religious meetings. More than anything, the sight of young boys and girls and old men and women picking cotton in the stifling summer heat brought slavery into sharp focus for Frank. He had spoken out against the practice before without much success, but now his soul burned with indignation at the very notion that one person should own another. He was especially concerned that some Methodists did not even think it a sin to own slaves. Frank was convinced that if Methodist believers didn't band together to speak out against slavery, God's blessings would depart from them.

In his journal on June 26, 1780, while traveling through North Carolina, Frank wrote in his journal, "There are many things that are painful to me, but cannot yet be removed, especially slave-keeping and its attendant circumstances. The Lord will certainly hear the cries of the oppressed, naked, starving creatures. O, my God, think on this land. Let not disaster come upon America. Amen."

Several southern Methodist preachers accompanied Frank on various legs of his journey around Virginia and North Carolina. One of them was Edward Bailey, who rode and preached with Frank from August to October. The two men were often ill with various fevers and sicknesses that Frank supposed resulted from spending so much time in low-lying, damp areas. At times both Frank and Edward appeared to be near death.

Eventually Frank was forced to leave Edward at the home of a sympathetic doctor near Lynchburg, Virginia. Nine days later Frank received word that his traveling companion had died. He wrote in his journal:

Here I received the melancholy tidings of the death of my companion and friend, Edward Bailey; it was very distressing to me; riding together so long had created a great sympathy between us. He died on Tuesday last, about five o'clock, in full confidence—he spoke to the last

and bore a testimony to the goodness of God.
He would sometimes get upon his knees in the
bed, weak as he was, and pray. . . . It was a sor-
rowful quarterly meeting for me, few people,
they lifeless, and my dear friend dead!

Harry Hosier, a twenty-five-year-old black man
from Fayetteville, North Carolina, whose master
had freed him from slavery, traveled with Frank.
Although Harry could not read or write, Frank was
amazed at what a dynamic preacher he was. In fact,
Harry was soon attracting larger crowds than Frank.
But Frank did not mind. He would often let Harry
do the preaching while he prayed that God would
touch the hearts of men and women through Harry's
words.

On September 3, 1780, Frank took time to think
back, noting in his journal:

This day nine years past I sailed from Bristol,
Old England. Ah, what troubles have I passed
through! what sickness! what temptations! But
I think, though I am grown more aged, I have
a better constitution, and more gifts, and I
think much more grace. I can bear disappoint-
ments and contradiction with greater ease.
Trials are before me, very great ones, but God
hath helped me hitherto. I can with greater
confidence trust him! And indeed, what have
any of us to trust in for the future, except the
living God?

Two months later, in November, Frank caught a ferryboat across the Susquehanna River in Maryland and set out for Dover, Delaware, where the quarterly conference of the northern Methodists was to be held. As he looked back over his journey through the South, Frank noted, "Within this six months, I have traveled, according to my computation, two thousand six hundred and seventy-one miles."

The remainder of 1780 passed quickly, and as the annual conference to be held in April 1781 approached, Frank felt a sense of dread. He had stern news to deliver to the conference. John Wesley had replied to the letter he had sent. In no uncertain terms the Methodist founder had stated that the Methodists in North America were to stick with the traditional Methodist ways of doing things. There were to be no allowances or exceptions made to the rules. Frank was concerned about how the southern Methodist preachers and Robert Strawbridge would react to John's response. While he had been in the colonies, Thomas Rankin had managed to rein in Robert so that he did not administer the sacraments to Methodist followers on his Maryland circuits. But with Thomas now returned to England, Robert was again agitating over the issue. Frank hoped the Methodists wouldn't end up dividing after all.

One thing was different at this conference than at the previous one. Back then Frank had been loved and trusted by the northern preachers but was relatively unknown to the southern preachers. But Frank's six hard months of riding the Methodist circuits in the

South had changed the equation. Many of the southern preachers had ridden with Frank on his journey and had come to appreciate him too. When the
conference voted on whether or not to accept John
Wesley's restrictions, most of the southern Methodist preachers sided with Frank. Several preachers,
including Robert Strawbridge, were not present at the
conference, but Frank hoped they too would accept
the decision and not resist his leadership in the matter. It was something Frank need not have been concerned about. Robert died unexpectedly a short time
after the conference. His death swept away the last
pocket of resistance to Frank's leadership and closed
the matter.

Following a preaching trip through western Virginia, Frank made his way to Philadelphia, arriving
there on October 12, 1781. It was the first time he had
visited the city in five years, and he found the place
abuzz with political conversation about the future of
the American colonies. While in Philadelphia, Frank
learned of the showdown going on between the British and the Continental army, reinforced with French
troops.

British forces under the command of British general Lord Cornwallis had occupied Yorktown, on the
York River in Virginia, a fortified position that could
be resupplied by sea. In response, George Washington had moved his army of American and French
soldiers to Virginia to oppose the British move. In
September the French navy defeated the British fleet
off the Virginia coast, cutting off General Cornwallis's

army from resupply and reinforcement as well as from an escape route.

At the time Frank heard the news, Washington had his troops besieging the British defenses. On October 19, seven days after Frank arrived in Philadelphia, General Cornwallis surrendered his entire army of over eight thousand men to George Washington. Like many people, Frank hoped this humiliating British defeat would signal the end of the war. While British troops still occupied New York City, Charleston, and Savannah, reports from England indicated that the British Parliament had lost the will to keep fighting. Frank prayed with all his heart that the fighting would end and the colonies would be at peace once again.

Chapter 11

So Strangely Set Free

As it turned out, the rumors were true. The British Parliament had tired of the war. In February 1782, the British House of Commons voted to end the war with the American colonies. In April, the British began peace talks in Paris, with John Adams and Benjamin Franklin representing the former British colonies in America.

It wasn't until May 10, 1782, while he was visiting Culpeper, Virginia, that Frank learned of the end of the fighting. He wrote in his journal, "Here I heard the good news that Britain had acknowledged the independence for which America has been contending— may it be so! The Lord does what to Him seemeth good."

Eleven days later, Frank attended the Methodist conference being held at Lovely Lane Chapel in Baltimore. A motion was put forward that called for "Brother Asbury to act according to Mr. Wesley's original appointment and preside over the American conferences and the whole work." The motion was carried unanimously. Francis Asbury was now the leader of all Methodists in North America.

After the conference, Frank was once again on horseback, riding the Methodist circuits to encourage society members and preachers alike. In 1783, with the expansion of settlements across the Allegheny Mountains in the west, he appointed Jeremiah Lambert as the first Methodist to cross the mountains and establish the Holston Methodist circuit in the region of the headwaters of the Tennessee River. Frank wanted to ride with Jeremiah across the Alleghenies, but he could not make the journey because of a severely ulcerated foot. Once his foot had healed, Frank continued to ride the circuits in both the North and the South.

As fall approached, Frank learned that on September 3, 1783, the Treaty of Paris had been signed between Great Britain and the new United States of America, formally ending the war and acknowledging the independence of the United States from Great Britain. With the war finally settled, Frank looked forward to 1784 and all of the hope and promise it held.

Throughout the war, despite the challenges of the revolution, the number of Methodist Societies and those attending them had stayed strong, even increasing in some areas, particularly Virginia and North Carolina. In 1780 there were forty-two Methodist preachers, twenty circuits, and 8,504 society members. But when the fighting ended, Methodism began to grow rapidly, until in 1784 there were eighty-three preachers, forty-six circuits, and fifteen thousand Methodist members. All of this kept Frank busy as he oversaw the growth and development of Methodism in the new United States. He was grateful for the caliber of the American-born preachers who had been raised up to ride the circuits and care for the spiritual well-being of those they served.

As he worked away, Frank waited patiently for news from his parents. They had written to him sporadically before the war, but he had not received a letter from them in seven years. Six years had passed since Frank had sent a letter home to them with George Shadford. Frank longed to hear how his parents were doing. He even wondered whether they were still alive. Then in June 1784, a letter arrived from Great Barr, England. Frank scanned the envelope as a wave of relief washed over him. He eagerly read the letter to learn that both his parents were still alive. They were now in their late sixties, and Frank's father was tired and worn and no longer able to work as a gardener at Hamstead Hall. Meanwhile, Eliza Asbury begged her son to come home and visit before she died and to write home more often now that the war was over.

Frank replied to the letter right away, telling his parents that he would not be leaving America to return to England anytime soon: "I am perfectly happy in the circumstances I am under; believing the hand of God has been signally displayed, in bringing me to and preserving me in America." He went on to say, "You want to see me. I make no doubt, as I do you. My constitution is now remarkably seasoned to the country. I enjoy an uncommon share of health, under much labour of body and mind. I trust my dear parents, you have not wanted yet. In my travels I visit the parents of preachers, and think so will others do to mine."

In regard to his mother's query as to whether her thirty-nine-year-old son was married yet, Frank explained that he was still single and intended to stay that way. He pointed out that the life of a traveling preacher's wife was not an easy one. Besides, he did not have the money to keep a family and send money home to his parents. There would be no grandchildren in the Asbury household, and no trip back to England in the foreseeable future. Frank concluded his letter by saying, "You think, 'Could I see my child again, I should be happy, and die in peace.' Yes, if I could stay with you, but how painful to part. I am under some thought that America will be my country for life."

About the same time that Frank received the letter from his parents, he received another from one of John Wesley's assistants, though this letter raised more questions than it answered. Instead of instructing Frank what to do next, the letter informed him that John was sending Dr. Thomas Coke to America with a very special mission. Frank had not met

Thomas, though he had heard of him. Thomas was an ordained Church of England minister who had been pushed out of his church in 1776 by parishioners unhappy with his Methodist sympathies. Thomas then became John Wesley's right-hand man. In fact, rumor had it that Thomas was being groomed to take eighty-one-year-old John Wesley's place when he died. Frank waited anxiously for word that Thomas had arrived in North America.

While Frank was traveling in Maryland, he received word that Thomas and two other men were in New York City. He arranged for the men to travel south to Delaware to meet some of the local American Methodist preachers. The meeting took place at Barratt's Chapel, ten miles south of Dover, Delaware, on the afternoon of November 14, 1784. Frank was running late by the time he made it to Barratt's Chapel. He had hoped to be early so he could greet Thomas before the meeting started, but his horse had thrown a shoe, forcing Frank to stop, find a blacksmith, and have the missing shoe replaced.

The meeting was already under way when Frank arrived at the large, square redbrick building. As he opened the side door to the chapel, Frank felt nervous. He was about to learn what the special mission was that John Wesley had for the Methodists in North America. Frank slid into a pew and waited for his eyes to adjust to the dim light. A short, stout man, whom Frank judged to be about his own age, was preaching from the pulpit. He spoke in a high-pitched voice with a Welsh accent.

"It's the Reverend Thomas Coke," the man next to Frank leaned over and whispered.

Frank nodded. He'd guessed as much. Two men were sitting beside the pulpit. As he squinted, Frank recognized one of them as Richard Whatcoat. Richard was twelve years older than Frank and had been a leader in the Methodist Society in Wednesbury, where Frank had preached many times as a member of Richard's Methodist band. Frank could hardly sit still throughout the rest of the meeting. He was eager to talk to Richard and hear any news he might have about Frank's parents and friends. Frank waited impatiently for Thomas to stop preaching, but when Thomas stopped, something strange happened. Frank watched as Richard and the other man took the communion cup and invited the hearers to come forward and take communion.

Frank was shocked as he watched the scene. As far as he was aware, Richard was not an ordained minister; only Thomas was. So why was Richard serving communion while Thomas watched? Frank sat back, trying to imagine why this was happening. These men had been sent out directly by John Wesley, yet they were going against John's express order that Methodist preachers were not to administer the sacraments. How could it be?

As soon as the meeting was over, Frank stepped forward to greet the newcomers. It was a wonderful moment when Frank and Richard embraced. "How good it is to see you!" Frank exclaimed. "We have been praying for news from England, and that you should bring it is an added blessing. Have you seen my parents recently?"

Richard grinned and nodded. "They are still living," he said. "Your dear mother still holds the door open for any Methodist preacher who comes by. Every night she prays for you."

"And I for her," Frank replied.

"Frank, this is Thomas Vasey," Richard said, introducing his partner in ministry.

As Frank embraced Richard's partner and welcomed him, he noticed Thomas Coke walking toward him. Frank reached out his arms and embraced him as well. "Brother Coke, I am Francis Asbury."

"I knew it was you," Thomas said. "What a joy to meet you."

"And you too," Frank replied. "I know we have much to talk about, especially after communion was administered this afternoon by Methodist preachers. But first, the Widow Barratt has invited us all to dinner. Let us eat together and then talk."

Frank, Thomas Coke, Thomas Vasey, and Richard joined a dozen other preachers for a delicious dinner. Afterward Frank and Thomas Coke slipped outside into the brisk evening air to continue their conversation.

"The truth is," Thomas confided in Frank, "John Wesley did everything he could to keep the American Methodists as part of the Church of England. He tried to convince Dr. Lowth, the bishop of London, to ordain some of the Methodist preachers, but he refused because they were not scholars."

"I see," Frank said, suddenly remembering that Thomas was a brilliant scholar himself with a doctorate in civil law from Oxford University.

Before Frank could think of something to say, Thomas went on. "Wesley spoke to the bishop quite plainly. He said 'It's not that I despise learning, I do not, but what is learning compared to piety? Does your lordship examine the applicants to see if they serve Christ or the devil? Whether they love God or the world? Whether they have any serious thoughts about heaven or hell?'"

"He is to the point," Frank said, happy to hear that John had lost none of his fire, even in old age.

"Yes," Thomas continued. "He didn't stop there either. When the bishop refused to consider ordaining any of our preachers, Brother Wesley wrote to him and said, 'Can you see your way to ordain any of our men to minister to the little flock in America? I note that your lordship does ordain men who know Greek and Latin but know no more about saving souls than of catching whales!'"

"I am sure that comment did not help the cause."

"The cause was lost by then, anyway. It was clear that we were not getting any help from the Church of England, so, as difficult as it was for John Wesley, he took the only route open to him," Thomas stated.

"And what might that be?"

"Just before we sailed, John Wesley ordained Richard Whatcoat and Thomas Vasey as elders and me as superintendent, well, co-superintendent, really. As soon as possible, I am to lay hands on you so that we can labor together as the co-superintendents of the Methodist Church in America."

Frank's head reeled. He was not so shocked to think that he might be chosen by John Wesley to lead the Methodist Societies in North America, but the Methodist Church!

"You did not use the word *society*," Frank pointed out to Thomas.

"No, I did not. In light of this extraordinary revolution, John Wesley has come to the conclusion that the cause of Christ can best be served by setting the Methodists in America free from the Church of England. They will have two superintendents—you and me—and we will be able to ordain anyone we please to serve communion and baptize others. Brother Wesley has sent some documents along with me. I am sure they will guide us well as we set up our church in America."

Frank could scarcely believe it. "I thought John Wesley would go to his grave being loyal to the Church of England," he blurted out. "To think he has cut us loose! It's hard to imagine."

"That it is," Thomas agreed, unfolding one of the documents. "But here it is quite clearly stated: 'As our American brethren are now totally disentangled, both from the State and the English hierarchy, we dare not entangle them again, either with the one or the other. They are now at full liberty simply to follow the Scriptures and the primitive Church. And we judge it best that they should stand fast in the liberty wherewith God has so strangely set them free.'"

"I never thought I would see this day," Frank said. "This is certainly an answer to prayer but not the answer I was expecting. The Methodists to the south will be very happy with this news. Now those preachers can carry out all the work of the Lord without hindrance. How extraordinary!"

"It is," Thomas agreed. "But it has not come without a price. It has caused quite a rift between John Wesley and his brother Charles, but John is convinced he has the Lord's mind on this and will not be swayed."

"What do we do now?" Frank asked.

"I would like to lay hands on you and ordain you, possibly tomorrow," Thomas replied.

Frank's head spun. There was so much to take in, but even so, one thought lodged in his mind: *If this is to be an American church, we must involve all the American preachers. This cannot be seen as something that the British Methodists have imposed on us.*

For a long while, Frank was silent before speaking again. He cleared his throat. "I think we had best start as we mean to continue, by involving the Americans in their own destiny. What say we call a meeting as soon as possible to discuss the future of the Methodists in America and put my ordination to the vote? If I have the support of both the northern and southern preachers, I will be honored for you to ordain me as coleader."

"You are a man of America, I am not," Thomas said. "I will agree to those terms. Yet it is a matter of some urgency. Where and when should we meet?"

Frank thought for a moment. It was mid-November. If a man left on horseback now, he could reach the most outlying areas in Virginia and the Carolinas in four weeks and take two weeks to get directly back again. "With God's help, I think we could be assembled by Christmas. Let's meet at Lovely Lane Chapel in Baltimore. It's central, and the roads there are still passable after snow."

And so it was agreed.

Later that night Frank asked Freeborn Garrettson to ride out the following morning, locate as many of the Methodist preachers as he could find, and urge them to meet in Baltimore at Christmas. He also arranged for Thomas Coke, Richard Whatcoat, and Thomas Vasey to see some of the American work before the conference. Harry Hosier would accompany them around a thousand-mile circuit that included much of Delaware, Maryland, and Virginia.

Later that evening Frank opened the document pouch Thomas Coke had given him. He realized that he was holding in his hands the founding documents of the first church denomination to be established in the United States of America. The documents consisted of a letter from John Wesley, instructions on how to order a church service, a list of twenty-four articles of faith, rituals for baptisms and for serving communion, and a hymnal. Frank settled into a straight-back wooden chair and began with the letter:

Bristol, September 10, 1784. I have accordingly appointed Dr. Coke and Mr. Francis Asbury to be Joint Superintendents over our brethren in North America, as also Richard Whatcoat and Thomas Vasey, to act as elders among them, by baptizing and administering the Lord's Supper. And I have prepared a Liturgy little differing from that of the Church of England (I think, the best constituted National Church in the world), which I advise all the traveling preachers to use on the Lord's Day in all the congregations, reading the Litany only on Wednesdays and Fridays and praying extempore on all other days. I also advise the elders to administer the Supper of the Lord on every Lord's Day.

If any one will point out a more rational and scriptural way of feeding and guiding those poor sheep in the wilderness, I will gladly embrace it. At present I cannot see any better method than that I have taken.

Frank put down the letter, bowed his head, and wept.

Chapter 12

An American Bishop

Frank looked at his pocket watch. It was exactly ten o'clock on the morning of Friday, December 24, 1784. He prayed silently as he looked around at the sixty preachers seated at the first session of the Christmas Conference in Lovely Lane Chapel in Baltimore. A sense of expectation filled the air. By now most of the preachers had heard the news. John Wesley had paved the way for Methodists in the United States to elect their own superintendent. It felt right to the participants. The war had freed their country from English rule, and now John Wesley was freeing them from domination by English ministers.

For his part, Frank still found it hard to believe that John Wesley had instructed them to form their own denomination. He remembered John telling him he would rather commit murder than serve communion without being an ordained minster. But times had changed, and John Wesley had changed with them.

As the meeting began, Thomas Coke stood and offered an opening prayer.

This is as it should be, Frank thought as Thomas prayed. *For now he is John Wesley's representative to us, but not for much longer.*

The first order of business at the conference was for Thomas Coke to read aloud the letter from John Wesley in which he released Methodists in North America from his leadership. This was followed by a discussion on what to call their new church. Several suggestions were offered before the group settled on the Methodist Episcopal Church. Frank was happy with the choice. Since they were already known as Methodists, it seemed a good idea for that to be the first word in their official name.

Next came long conversations over the structure of the church. As members of the Church of England, the Methodist preachers had firmly believed that God had set the king over them as their spiritual leader, and they were willing to submit to him. But what now? The questions flowed. How would they know whom God wanted to put over them? Was it appropriate to hold a vote for this person? Should they limit how long the person would be in office, or was it for life? Did the act of voting make it seem more like man's appointment than God's choice? Who should be in charge of what, and who should be answerable to whom?

These were difficult questions to work through, but after long, serious conversation, the men made progress. They started at the bottom with the unordained lay preachers. These men would establish and maintain circuits, with the goal of constantly expanding their evangelism to bring new areas under the influence of Methodism. Each lay preacher would make his way around his circuit once every two weeks, preaching and teaching at a different place each day. Once a quarter the local preachers would gather for a two-day meeting. At this meeting the offering money they had collected while circuit riding would be turned in, and there would be preaching, praying, singing, testifying, exhorting, and a love feast.

An elder would be responsible for organizing the quarterly meeting and overseeing the work of the lay preachers. He could baptize people and serve them communion. He would also travel around each circuit under his oversight once a quarter, encouraging the preachers and helping them with their congregations. It was decided that Thomas Coke should ordain twelve elders, who would be the equivalent of Church of England priests. Frank was one of those chosen to be ordained as an elder.

One of the others chosen to be ordained as an elder was William Black, a Yorkshire man living in Nova Scotia. William had written to John Wesley asking for help in establishing Methodist Societies throughout Nova Scotia. John had written back, suggesting that William attend the American conference where Thomas Coke was authorized to ordain him.

Following the ordination of the elders on Christmas Day, Frank had a long conversation with William Black. William was twenty-four years old and reminded Frank of himself when he was younger. While William had had little formal education in his youth, he now had a drive to make up for this lack. He was teaching himself Latin and Greek and systematically studying the Bible. Frank listened attentively as William explained how he had been converted five years before and then started preaching when he was twenty years old. He had read everything he could get his hands on written by John Wesley, and he tried hard to follow the Methodist way. William had created his own circuit among the scattered hamlets around the bays of Nova Scotia. He encouraged his converts to form bands and pointed them in the direction of whatever Christian church existed in the area. Frank was not alone in admiring the dedication of this lone Methodist preacher in Nova Scotia. In fact, the conference voted to send two of their strongest preachers, Freeborn Garrettson and James Cromwell, to Nova Scotia to assist William. The conference also ordained Jeremiah Lambert and assigned him to go as a Methodist preacher to Antigua in the West Indies.

As the discussion of the formation of the Methodist Episcopal Church continued, it was agreed that all men employed by the new church, whether they be preachers, elders, or bishops, should receive the same salary of sixty-four dollars a year. This meant there would be no pressure for a preacher to accept or reject a posting based upon the money he would be paid. Frank was happy with the yearly amount. He had few needs beyond food, clothing, and keeping his horse fed.

Later in the day a vote was taken to determine who would be the superintendents of the church, or bishops, as the conference members had decided they should be called. Both Frank and Thomas Coke were unanimously elected. The following day Frank prepared himself to be ordained as the coleader of the new denomination. His friend William Otterbein, a German minister, assisted Thomas Coke in the ceremony.

Frank was nervous as he knelt at the front of the church while Thomas laid his hands on him and said, "Know all men by these presents, that I, Thomas Coke, Doctor of Civil Law; late of Jesus College, in the University of Oxford, Presbyter of the Church of England, and Superintendent of the Methodist Episcopal Church in America; under the protection of Almighty God, and with a single eye to his glory; by the imposition of my hands, and prayer . . . set apart the said Francis Asbury for the office of a superintendent in the said Methodist Episcopal Church, a man whom I judge to be well qualified for that great work. And I do hereby recommend him to all whom it may concern, as a fit person to preside over the flock of Christ."

As Frank stood, he arose as Bishop Francis Asbury, a designation that he, trained to be buckle maker and with three years of schooling, never imagined would be possible.

With the task of ordination complete, the conference began to look at other pressing issues, of which there were many.

The first issue to be dealt with was one that had haunted Frank for a long time—slavery. Two black delegates were present at the conference. Richard Allen, a twenty-five-year-old Methodist preacher, had been born a slave in Philadelphia but ended up in Delaware when his family was sold to a plantation owner there. While still a slave, Richard had become a Christian after his master allowed him to attend Methodist meetings in the area. Later Richard was able to strike a deal with his master and work for his freedom. Now, as a freed slave, he was an enthusiastic Methodist preacher who had ridden circuits in Maryland, Pennsylvania, and Delaware. On a number of occasions Frank had ridden circuits with Richard. The second black delegate at the conference was Harry Hosier, the dynamic preacher who had traveled with Frank when he visited all the circuits in the South four years earlier.

Frank started the conversation about slavery by telling the preachers that he believed slavery was a terrible sin, one for which God would judge the United States if it did not change its laws. Thomas Coke agreed that slavery was a great stain on the new country, and he wanted the Methodists to take strong action against it right away. He urged everyone present to vote for the new Methodist Episcopal Church to take a public stand against the practice, denouncing anyone who owned slaves.

Frank was a little less sure of this path. He had ridden the circuits in Virginia and the Carolinas and knew how entitled many white people felt about owning slaves. Without slaves the entire lifestyle of the South would have to change, and many people feared such change. Frank thought it wiser to take a slower, less aggressive approach to the practice, but Thomas insisted on pushing for radical measures. Much as Frank expected, Thomas's stance drew a lot of argument, especially from some of the southern preachers. A number of these preachers felt that God had given them the right to own slaves and resented Englishmen telling them it was wrong to do so.

Everyone seemed to have an opinion on the matter. Some of the southern delegates pointed out that slaves were viewed as economic assets, much like horses or cows, and freeing them would mean losing a lot of money. Others said slaves needed time to adjust to the idea of freedom. They needed a plan to work toward so they would not be left destitute and homeless when given their freedom.

Nonetheless, the preachers were Methodists first, and they knew that the decisions they made at this first Christmas Conference would set the tone of the new church for decades to come. In what Frank viewed as a miracle, they talked and prayed until they came to an agreement. It was a radical plan intended as an example for all American slave owners to follow.

The agreement that the conference hammered out decreed that no one could remain a Methodist

without a plan to free any slaves he owned. Every
Methodist slave owner was given one year to sign
a plan that promised that every slave between ages
forty and forty-five would be freed upon reaching
forty-five. Those between the ages of twenty-five
and forty would be freed within five years, and those
between twenty and twenty-five would be freed by
age thirty. Those younger than twenty had to be freed
by the time they were twenty-five. Within ten years,
no Methodists would own slaves.

As the Christmas Conference moved into the sev-
enth day, the discussion turned to an idea Frank had
been considering for quite a while—a school for the
sons of Methodist preachers. Frank thought it was
best for preachers to be single men, as he was, free
from having to worry about money and family matters. But in truth, a number of his preachers wanted
to marry and continue circuit riding. This would put
a strain on their wives, especially when children were
born. Without a father at home, the children were
in danger of becoming unruly and undisciplined,
which, as far as Frank was concerned, would not do
for the children of a Methodist preacher.

To help the families of Methodist preachers cope,
Frank dreamed of a boys' school modeled on John
Wesley's Kingswood School near Bristol, England.
In that school, strict discipline was maintained, and
the boys had the opportunity to learn practical skills
along with book learning.

Several wealthy Methodists had already donated
land near Abingdon, Maryland, for such a school

along with a sum of money to help build it. However, Francis Asbury and Thomas Coke imagined two very different schools. Thomas's school was more like a college, teaching advanced Latin and Greek and grooming young men to be gentlemen. Frank was more motivated to produce hardy, horse-riding Methodist preachers. The two men described their different visions for a school to the conference delegates, and in the end Thomas's vision won their support.

Although this was not Frank's original dream, he was happy to go along with the changed plan. He knew how it felt to be embarrassed about a lack of education and how difficult it was to learn Latin and Greek. The delegates voted to begin erecting a three-story building on the site and find two well-educated teachers, possibly from England, to oversee the boys.

As soon as the conference was over, Frank set out to help the newly appointed elders arrange their circuits. He seemed to be everywhere. In less than three months, he toured Maryland, Virginia, and as far south as Charleston, South Carolina. Along the way he met with many Methodists, baptizing those who had not yet been baptized in the Church of England and serving them communion.

On May 26, 1785, Frank met up with Thomas Coke in Alexandria, Virginia, to attend a conference of the Methodist leaders of the state. Following up on the slavery issue, during this conference a petition was drafted calling for the "immediate or Gradual Extirpation of Slavery." The petition stated, "Justice, mercy, and truth, every virtue that can adorn the Man or the Christian, the Interest of the State, and the Welfare of Mankind, do unanswerably—uncontrollably plead for the removal of this grand Abomination." As the preachers spread out across Virginia, they would present the petition for people to sign. It was agreed that Frank and Thomas would also present a copy of the petition to George Washington and ask him to sign it.

Together the two bishops of the Methodist Episcopal Church set out toward Mount Vernon to visit George Washington, who had resigned as commander-in-chief of the Continental army seventeen months before. Frank had heard that Washington was sympathetic to the idea of abolishing slavery in the new country and wanted to enlist his support. He was hopeful that Washington would persuade members of the US Congress to abolish slavery as they made new laws for the United States.

With a firm handshake, Washington welcomed the two bishops into his lavish home at Mount Vernon on the bank of the Potomac River. The preachers were treated to a wonderful dinner, after which they sat on the porch and looked out on the river. In this beautiful setting Frank presented Washington with the petition calling for the abolition of slavery in Virginia. He urged Washington to sign it, but that was a tall order, since Washington himself owned slaves and relied on them to keep his home running and his farm productive. Still, Frank sensed that Washington could see the problems with allowing slavery to continue, not only in Virginia but also in the rest of the country, and that in his heart he sincerely wanted change. Washington politely refused to sign the petition, but he did agree to present it to the Virginia Assembly.

The result was not the one they had hoped for, and Frank left Mount Vernon with a heavy heart. He was greatly impressed by George Washington. Yet he feared for the future of the country if its citizens continued owning people as if they were mere cattle. Frank promised himself that he would keep fighting to end slavery and would encourage the free black Methodists to preach to slaves. As slaves, their bodies might be in bondage, but Frank longed for them all to know that their souls were free to worship God.

Chapter 13

Forward!

The weeks following the visit to George Washington were busy for Frank. Almost immediately Thomas Coke returned to England to take care
of other Methodist business. Besides overseeing
the Methodist work in North America with Frank,
Thomas oversaw the Methodist work in Ireland.
Thomas's departure left Frank to single-handedly
oversee the new Methodist Episcopal Church. One
of Frank's first official acts was to lay the cornerstone
for the new college being built in Abingdon, Maryland. The conference had elected to call the school
Cokesbury—a combination of Coke and Asbury—in
honor of the two bishops.

In his new position, Frank had been furnished a
clerical robe, which he wore to the event. But even

as he laid the new cornerstone, he felt out of place in the robe. Before long Frank stopped wearing it altogether. He was much more at home dressed like the people he served, in a plain pair of knee breeches, shirt, waistcoat, frock coat, and broad-rimmed hat. Frank stored his robe at Perry Hall, the Goughs' home outside Baltimore. Since he had no fixed home of his own, the Goughs had insisted that a room of their home be set aside for Frank. He was grateful to have somewhere to keep his journals and records of the meetings he attended.

With the cornerstone at Cokesbury laid, Frank climbed back onto a horse and set out to do the work he was called to do—riding the circuits and encouraging and organizing preachers. Wherever he went, Frank saw possibilities. He told his preachers, "We must reach every section of America—especially the raw frontiers. We must not be afraid of men, devils, wild animals, or disease. Our motto must always be *Forward!*"

Of course, Frank knew that this was a hard message. Records showed that half of the Methodist preachers died before they reached thirty years of age. Frank, who was now forty years old, often felt his life would soon be over. As a result, he was determined to make every minute count for God.

As 1786 began, Frank found himself in Charleston, South Carolina, where he took time to write to his parents. By now he realized that he would never return to England. His heart belonged to the United States, and he was sure that was where he would labor until his death. Nonetheless, he felt a strong sense of obligation to his parents and regularly sent them half of his meager pay. He hoped the money would be enough to feed and keep them in their old age. To his parents he wrote, "If Providence will so dispose of us as that we shall not see each other in time, let us live for eternity, and labor to meet in Glory. . . . Remember for many years, I lived with and labored and prayed for you. I at this distance of time and place, care for and send to your relief, and cease not night and day to pray for you, who am as ever your most unworthy but dutiful son in the Lord."

From Charleston, Frank headed north to western Virginia and entered the Ohio River Valley, where the Redstone circuit had been established the year before. This circuit, which took six weeks to ride, had continued to grow and now had thirty preaching spots. In this sparsely populated area, many pioneers had come to rely on Methodist preachers as their only source of spiritual guidance. They waited eagerly for a preacher to come and perform weddings and baptisms. As a result, Methodist preachers had gained the reputation of going where no other religious groups would go. As one observer wryly noted, "If they were welcomed, they made Methodists of everyone in sight. If they were opposed, they did the same. If they were ignored, they did the same." A common saying had developed: "The weather is so bad today that nothing's out but crows and Methodist preachers." Frank smiled when he heard this saying for the first time. Nothing made him more proud than to know that his "cavalry of preachers" was doing its job.

Traveling back through Virginia on his way to Baltimore, Frank learned that George Washington had honored his word and presented the Methodists' petition calling for the end of slavery in the state to the Virginia Assembly. Unfortunately, the assembly failed to even read the petition, much less act upon it. Frank was disappointed. He'd hoped for more. Yet he had done his best on the issue, and he would not stop raising it whenever he could. He longed for the day when every citizen of the United States would be free.

As superintendent, Frank had arranged three conferences for the Methodist preachers during 1787. The first would be held in Salisbury, North Carolina, on May 17; the second in Petersburg, Virginia, on June 19; and the third in Abingdon, Maryland, on July 24. But on September 6, 1786, Frank received a letter from Thomas Coke, who was still in England. In his letter Thomas set earlier dates for the three conferences Frank had planned. He also included quoted instructions from John Wesley in the letter: "I desire that you would appoint a General Conference of all our preachers in the United States to meet at Baltimore on May 1, 1787, and that Mr. Richard Whatcoat may be appointed superintendent with Mr. Francis Asbury." The letter went on to say that John Wesley also wanted Freeborn Garrettson, who had recently returned from two years serving in Nova Scotia, to be appointed superintendent of the Methodist work there.

Frank was appalled when he read the letter, not because he thought appointing Richard Whatcoat or Freeborn Garrettson to the various positions was a bad idea, but because John Wesley felt it was his right to call a meeting in the United States and appoint superintendents. Richard's appointment as superintendent, Frank suspected, was a first step in recalling Frank to England. But Frank knew the American preachers better than Thomas Coke did, and he was sure that they would not agree to someone in England, even John Wesley, telling them what to do.

Thomas Coke arrived back in North America just in time for the conference on May 1, 1787. Just as Frank had predicted, the American preachers were indignant at Thomas and the notion that Methodist leaders in England thought they could make decisions for Methodists in the United States. They scolded Thomas and insisted that he sign a statement acknowledging he could make decisions regarding American Methodists only when he was present in the country. Like Frank, the conference attendees were suspicious that elevating Richard to the position of superintendent was the first step in recalling Frank to England, which none of them wanted to happen. As a result, they refused to appoint Richard to the position. And Freeborn refused to be appointed as the superintendent of the Methodist work in Nova Scotia unless the Canadian preachers voted and elected him to that position.

In the end, the conference voted to appoint Freeborn as the elder overseeing the Methodist circuits on the Delmarva Peninsula, occupied by most of Delaware and portions of Maryland and Virginia. The conference delegates went even further, affirming a resolution that stated the Methodist Episcopal Church in the United States was to be governed solely by people appointed in the United States.

Following the conference in Baltimore, the Methodist preachers returned to ride their circuits with new vigor, which translated into more and more circuits being added. At the start of 1786 there were fifty-one Methodist circuits, but as 1788 approached, that number had risen to seventy-six. All of this growth kept Frank busy overseeing the work, as Thomas Coke had once again departed for England. Not only were there more circuits for Frank to ride and watch over, but there were also new preachers for him to recruit and appoint to these circuits. In fact, the number of preachers during this period rose from 117 to 165.

Still, as busy as he was, Frank took the time to attend the three-day opening celebration of Cokesbury College in December 1787. The new wooden building was three stories high, 40 feet wide, and 108 feet long, with lots of windows on each floor. It had been decided that the sons of traveling preachers and Methodist orphan boys should be boarded, educated, and clothed for free at the college, and a boy had to be seven years of age to be enrolled. By the time of the opening celebration, twenty-five male students were enrolled. They were supervised by two teachers, the Reverend Levi Heath, whom Thomas Coke had recruited from England, and Truman Marsh, a recent graduate of Yale College.

The rules for Cokesbury College were practical and covered matters such as bedding, bathing, recreation, and schoolwork. Each student was to have a bed to himself, and the boys were to sleep on mattresses, not feather beds, since mattresses were deemed to be healthier. The school was equipped with a bath, and the students were to bathe regularly, one at a time, and were not to remain in the bath water for more than a minute. The boys were also forbidden to bathe in the nearby river. Suitable outdoor recreation was defined as gardening, walking, or riding, while indoor recreation consisted of working in the woodworking shop. And there was to be no play. The rules clearly stated, "The students shall be indulged with nothing which the world calls play. Let this rule be observed with the strictest nicety, for those who play when they are young will play when they are old. Idleness or any other fault may be punished with confinement."

To make sure there was no room for idleness, the students followed a strict routine. They were to arise at five o'clock each morning and assemble at six o'clock for public prayer. At seven o'clock they ate breakfast, and from eight until midday they attended classes. Lunch was at one o'clock in the afternoon, after which they were given time for recreation. From three to six o'clock they were to attend classes again, followed directly by supper. At seven o'clock in the evening they were to gather for public prayer once more. Without fail, they were to be in their beds by nine o'clock. As far as Frank was concerned, the rules were splendid, just what was needed to shape the boys into mature Christian young men.

Following the opening of Cokesbury College, Frank set out to visit the various Methodist preachers and see how their circuits were going. He traveled through Virginia and Maryland and then made his way to New York and on into New England.

Often someone would ask Frank why he didn't stay in one place and let the traveling preachers come to him with their reports. His answer was threefold. First, he loved to preach to those who had not heard the gospel. Second, he wanted to get to know all of the Methodist preachers to make sure he assigned them the right circuits. And third, he wanted to be an example. Frank knew he was asking a lot from his preachers, who were to stay poor and single (if possible) and constantly be on the move. The least he felt he could do as their leader was to model what he asked them to do.

After visiting New York and New England, Frank made his way to Charleston, South Carolina. On this trip Frank crossed into Georgia for the first time. In April 1788 he made his first trip across the Smoky Mountains. He began this leg of his journey in Morganton, North Carolina, and followed the French Broad River, eventually making it all the way to Bristol in the Southwest Territory (Tennessee). The weather was terrible during the trip. It rained nearly all the way, but Frank seldom stopped for rain or even for thunderstorms. The houses he stayed in were tiny log cabins with dirt floors and little heat. Sometimes there was so little heat in the houses that Frank's clothes were still wet when he set out to ride again the following morning.

Frank slept on every type of bed imaginable on his trips, often sharing a bed with two or three other people and a host of bedbugs and fleas. Sometimes the people he stayed with were embarrassed by having so little food to offer. But Frank happily ate whatever they ate, even if it was corn mush or a cup of tea for dinner. As he made his way along, Frank knew he was blazing a trail for other preachers to follow, and he felt it was a privilege to be invited into the poorest of homes. At each place he was invited to stay he always prayed with the family and told the children Bible stories. When he left, most hosts asked that he or another Methodist preacher come back again.

In late July 1788, Frank crossed the mountains into western Pennsylvania and traveled to Uniontown, where the first Methodist Conference west of the mountains was to be held. By August 10, he was back in Baltimore, attending a conference there. By then Frank was tired. The Baltimore conference was his sixth conference that year, with each conference being held in a different state. But tired as he was, there was little time for rest. Following the conference in Baltimore, Frank headed for Pennsylvania, New Jersey, New York, and Delaware before returning to Maryland. As he traveled, Frank's biggest concern was finding enough suitable preachers to ride the ever-increasing number of circuits in the growing country. During 1788 alone, 11,500 people had joined the Methodist Church.

In March 1789, Thomas Coke returned to America and joined Frank in Charleston, South Carolina, where he was presiding over the Methodist

conference there. Thomas brought with him a bundle
of letters. Among them was a letter from John Wesley
dated September 20, 1788. The letter was a response
to the 1787 conference in Baltimore that had failed to
follow John's express instructions. He had wanted to
send Freeborn Garrettson back to Nova Scotia and
elevate Richard Whatcoat to superintendent in the
United States. Frank's heart sank as he read:

> There is, indeed, a wide difference between the
> relationship wherein you stand to the Ameri-
> cans and the relationship wherein I stand to
> all Methodists. You are the elder brother of
> the American Methodists; I am under God the
> father of the whole family. Therefore, I natu-
> rally care for you in a manner no other person
> can do. . . .
>
> But in one point, my dear brother, I am
> afraid both the Doctor and you differ from
> me. I study to be little; you study to be great.
> I creep; you strut along. I [founded] a school,
> you a college! . . . Nay, and you call it after
> your own names.
>
> One instance of this, of your greatness, has
> given me great concern. How can you, how
> dare you, suffer yourself to be called Bishop? I
> shudder, I start at the very thought! Men may
> call me a knave or a fool, a rascal, a scoundrel,
> and I am content, but they shall never by my
> consent call me a Bishop! For my sake, and for
> God's sake, for Christ's sake, put a full end to
> this!

Frank could hardly believe that the man he had loved and followed his whole life had written to him in such a manner. It was a bitter pill for him to swallow. Despite his feelings, Frank prayed he would bear them gracefully and remain loyal in his heart to John Wesley and his methods. He realized that John was now old and could not grasp the democratic way of doing things that had taken root in the United States. Yes, they had founded a college and it was named after him and Thomas. Yes, he was called Bishop. And yes, the Methodists in America had not followed Wesley's express instructions. But in each instance, conferences of Methodist leaders in the United States had voted that those decisions be made. Frank had only followed their wishes.

The previous year, a new constitution for the United States had been ratified. And while Frank and Thomas headed north from Charleston on April 30, 1789, George Washington was being inaugurated in New York City as the first president under the new constitution.

On May 24, 1789, the two bishops were together at the John Street Church in New York for a conference. During the conference they were charged with writing a note of congratulations to George Washington on becoming president. That night Frank and Thomas worked on the letter and expressed their confidence in Washington's leadership to preserve and protect both civil and religious liberty. The next day they presented the letter to the conference attendees for approval. Following approval, Frank and Thomas gave it to Washington in person.

In his official response to the letter, Washington thanked Frank and Thomas and the Methodist Episcopal Church for their affection. He then went on to state, "It shall be my endeavor to manifest the purity of my inclinations for promoting the happiness of mankind, as well as the sincerity of my desire to contribute whatever may be in my power toward the civil and religious liberties of the American people. In pursuing this line of conduct, I hope, by the assistance of Divine Providence, not altogether to disappoint the confidence which you have been pleased to repose in me."

In presenting their letter to George Washington, the Methodist Episcopal Church became the first denomination in the United States to congratulate the new president and wish him well.

Frank left New York hoping that Washington could live up to all that he had proposed. But the truth was that the new government of the United States was already squabbling over who had more power—the states or the federal government. The Methodist Episcopal Church was facing similar issues. The church was growing rapidly, and governing it was a challenge.

Frank was attending ten conferences a year now. At each one he had to lay out all the issues the Methodist church faced, so that the attendees of all ten conferences could vote and reach a universal consensus. As a result, Frank had proposed that a council be set up instead, consisting of the bishops and elders who would meet together and vote on matters regarding the running of the church. Both Frank and Thomas

thought this a much more efficient way to admin-
istrate than having each conference hear and vote
on the issues. However, James O'Kelly, a Methodist
elder in Virginia, opposed this approach. He believed
that a general conference should be called, at which
the preachers could have a democratic say in the
decisions made for the church, rather than have decisions dictated by a nonelected council. He pointed
out that Frank could dominate such a council since
he had veto power over their decisions.

While Frank was aware of the debate regarding
the council, he had something more pressing calling
him—the West—over the mountains. While Thomas
left New York to return to England after the conference, Frank headed along Forbes Road, one of the
two main routes pioneers took across the mountains
in Pennsylvania. He was on his way to the settlement
of Pittsburgh, with a population of four hundred, to
visit a new circuit that had been established there.

By early 1790, Frank was back in Charleston,
South Carolina, for a conference. He then traveled to
Georgia for another conference. Traveling in Georgia
was not easy, especially in the backcountry, but Frank
persevered, preaching in a different place each night.
As he rode, Frank sang hymns or quoted from the
New Testament, most of which he knew by heart.

Methodist preachers had pushed into Kentucky
and established circuits there, and they wrote and
asked Frank to visit and ride the circuits with them.
Frank was eager to go, and he set out from North
Carolina with Richard Whatcoat for Tennessee,

intending to travel on to Kentucky. But because he was exhausted from his traveling and the conferences he had been attending, he fell ill along the way and could not go on. Instead Frank and Richard detoured to western Virginia and the home of Elizabeth Russell, a gracious Methodist woman, so that Frank could rest and recuperate. Richard stayed with Frank in Virginia.

During their stay at Elizabeth's home, Frank and Richard decided that it would be best if they did not try to make it to Kentucky at this time. However, that first night Frank had a vivid dream in which a group of men, including two preachers, came to accompany him through the mountains. Frank was not sure whether he should take this dream seriously, but the next day a group of ten men, including two preachers, Peter Massie and Hope Hull, arrived from Kentucky at Elizabeth's home. Frank knew that God wanted him to travel at this time.

In all, sixteen men, including the ten from Kentucky, Frank and Richard, and four others, set out on the trail. Because it would be a dangerous ride through country where Indians had been ambushing and killing people, the group carried thirteen rifles and ample gunpowder with them. Frank himself consented to carry a powder horn, on the side of which he carved the date of departure, May 1, 1790.

The group made their way into North Carolina, where they joined the Wilderness Road, a trail that led through the Cumberland Gap and on into Kentucky. The difficult ride had the group climbing mountains, fording deep rivers, and crossing muddy streams. Despite the difficult conditions on the trail, the men kept a fast pace, covering about fifty miles a day. Because of the threat of Indian attack, no one wanted to linger. Seeing the graves of twenty-four pioneers massacred and scalped by Indians helped Frank understand the danger of traveling in these parts—danger the preachers on this circuit faced regularly. When the group stopped to camp at night, Frank usually slept only an hour or two at a time, awakening instantly to any unfamiliar sound in the dark.

As the men rode into Kentucky, many of the people Frank encountered were lonely and scared. They recounted tales of family members killed by Indians or wives and daughters carried away by them. They also told Frank how much the Methodist preachers meant to them. They knew the preachers were risking their lives to visit and pray with them. Frank also noted how this risk had built a strong loyalty between the preachers and the frontierspeople. Often a group of men from one outpost would escort the preacher to his next post, keeping him safe from harm.

Frank was in for a surprise when the group reached Lexington, Kentucky. He found Charles White, who had been a trustee of Wesley Chapel in New York City, living there. Frank had dined with Charles on numerous occasions back then, but because of his Loyalist sympathies, Charles had been forced to flee to Nova Scotia. Eventually Charles had made his way west and ended up in Lexington.

While in Lexington, Frank and Richard held a conference for the local Methodists and began plans to build a school. They decided the school would be named Bethel. After ending the conference and spending time riding the circuit, preaching from farm to farm and cabin to cabin, Frank headed east over the mountains to North Carolina. Another busy conference schedule awaited him there.

A group of fifty people, twenty of them armed with rifles, accompanied Frank and Richard back down the Wilderness Road. On June 2, 1790, they reached the McKnights' residence on the Yadkin River in North Carolina. The Methodist preachers had been waiting anxiously for several days for Frank to arrive. When Frank and Richard rode up, tired and bedraggled, a joyful group of preachers ran to meet them.

"We thought you were dead!" one of the preachers declared.

Chapter 14

Fishing with a Large Net

The Methodist Episcopal Church was on the rise. By 1790 it had over fifty-seven thousand members, having more than doubled in size in three years. The church now had circuits in all thirteen of the United States as well as routes in the frontier territories and two sections of Canada. The growth kept Frank busy traveling, preaching, and presiding over conferences.

In April 1791, Thomas Coke again returned to the United States and joined Frank for the General Conference in Baltimore. Frank hoped that Thomas would help in addressing the growing problem with some of the southern Methodist preachers, led by James O'Kelly. James had continued to stir up opposition to Frank by claiming that Frank was telling the preachers what to do and where to ride circuits rather than asking them what they would prefer.

Frank was disturbed to learn that Thomas had experienced a change of heart and now supported the position of the southern group against the council. Then Frank discovered that Thomas was secretly writing to Bishop William White of the Protestant Episcopal Church (the post-revolutionary name of the Church of England in the United States). Thomas's letters suggested that John Wesley was sorry he had authorized the American Methodists to leave the Church of England to form their own denomination and now wanted American Methodists to rejoin the Protestant Episcopal church. Frank was shocked by this turn of events, but he refused to become bitter about the matter. He wrote in his journal, "I see and hear many things that might wound my spirit if it were not that the Lord bears me up above all."

While Frank was still trying to work out how to respond to Thomas's secret correspondence with Bishop White, news arrived from England that John Wesley had died. Frank was deeply saddened and wrote in his journal:

> The solemn news reached our ears that the public papers had announced the death of that dear man of God, John Wesley. He died in his own house in London, in the eighty-eighth year of his age, after preaching the gospel sixty-four years. . . . I conclude, his equal is not to be found among all the sons he hath brought up, nor his superior among

all the sons of Adam he may have left behind. Brother Coke was sunk in spirit, and wished to hasten home immediately. For [me], notwithstanding my long absence from Mr. Wesley, and a few unpleasant expressions in some of the letters the dear old man has written to me (occasioned by the misrepresentations of others), I feel the stroke most sensibly; and, I expect, I shall never read his works without reflecting on the loss which the church of God and the world has sustained by his death.

Sure enough, upon hearing the news, Thomas set out immediately for England, since he expected to be named as John Wesley's successor.

Following the death of John Wesley and the abrupt departure of Thomas Coke, Frank heard no more about the secret plans for the merging of the Methodist Episcopal Church and the Protestant Episcopal Church in the United States. But other things threatened the heart of American Methodism.

One challenge was the number of black people becoming Methodists. Between 1786 and 1788 their numbers in the Methodist Church went from 1,890 to 6,545, and the number continued to grow steadily from there. Many of these people were slaves, and Frank welcomed every one of them into the church as brothers and sisters. But not everyone else was so inclusive. There was friction within the church, particularly in Philadelphia, where the number of black people attending St. George's grew so rapidly that it overwhelmed the seating capacity.

In 1792 a balcony was added to accommodate the growing numbers of people attending services. This was when the trouble started. Some of the white deacons in the church decided that black people should occupy the balcony while white people sat in the pews on the main floor. However, not all of the black people who showed up for service on the Sunday morning that the balcony opened were aware of this arrangement. Many of them streamed onto the main floor and sat where they normally sat. As the service opened they all knelt to pray as usual. But as they knelt, one of the white trustees of the church grabbed Absalom Jones, a gifted black Methodist preacher, by the shoulder and tried to drag him to his feet. "You must get up. You cannot kneel here," the trustee said.

"Wait until the prayer is over," Absalom said quietly.

"No, you must get up now or I will call for help and force you to move," the trustee responded.

"Please wait until the prayer is over," Absalom repeated.

The trustee and several other men then tried to forcibly move Absalom and the other black members of the congregation to the segregated balcony. The sound reverberated through the sanctuary as an elder prayed at the front of the church. As soon as the elder had finished, Absalom stood and, joined by fellow preacher Richard Allen, led the group out of the church. They never returned to St. George's.

When Frank heard the report of the walkout, he was sad. Because he lived a Christian creed that declared all men are brothers and equal before God, it was hard for him to accept that one group of Methodists would treat another group so badly simply because of the color of their skin. He also heard that Richard was now leading a group of those who had walked out of St. George's and who followed Methodist principles. Frank wondered whether black people might be better off with their own Methodist churches.

In April 1792, Frank was in the saddle again, this time headed back to Kentucky. In Lexington he preached, held a conference, and inspected the new Bethel School he had helped plan during his visit two years before. While in Kentucky he tried to keep his mind on his mission, but, as he wrote in his journal, he was easily distracted: "I . . . hear so much about Indians, convention, treaty, killing, and scalping that my attention is drawn more to these things than I would wish." Despite the continued threat of Indian attack, Frank enjoyed a fruitful time preaching in and around Lexington and encouraging the Christians of the settlement.

Frank rode into Baltimore on November 1, 1792, just in time for the first General Conference. However, he had become so ill that he could not attend meetings. Thankfully, Thomas Coke had recently returned from England and was able to take charge of the conference. Each night one of Frank's friends brought him a report about what was discussed. Since he couldn't attend the meetings, Frank wrote a letter to conference delegates, outlining the reasons why he believed he should have the power to appoint preachers to their circuits. When the matter came to a vote, James O'Kelly lost. He stormed out of the meeting, announcing that he was done with the Methodist Church. Several other preachers followed him. When Frank heard about this, he was not surprised, but he was upset to lose some of the southern preachers. He felt that two of these preachers in particular, William McKendree and Jesse Lee, had been promising preachers whose leadership gifts could have helped strengthen the church.

As soon as he was well enough to get out of bed again, Frank continued his never-ending circuit riding. He still tried to travel a little with all of the preachers, but this was becoming more and more difficult, since there were now 217 preachers serving over sixty thousand Methodist members.

In October 1793, Frank found himself traveling east to Philadelphia while most people were headed west, away from the city and the yellow fever epidemic raging there.

Frank was not afraid of death, which was a good thing, because ten percent of the population of the city had already died from the disease. Many more probably would have died if not for Richard Allen and Absalom Jones (now a leader of the black Methodists in Philadelphia). Because it was incorrectly believed by many that black people were immune to yellow fever, the two black Christian leaders in the city had rallied their followers to care for sick and dying white people. They also helped bury the dead.

When Frank arrived in Philadelphia, he met with Richard and Absalom and joined them in arranging help for those who needed it.

As Frank worked alongside Richard and Absalom, he was encouraged by the way both men were deeply committed to the spiritual needs of their people. Absalom was building a Methodist church called St. Thomas's for his followers, and Richard was building a church that he planned to call Bethel. Because of the yellow fever outbreak, the building programs of both churches had been put on hold. By the following July, however, Bethel African Methodist Episcopal Church was finished. Richard invited Frank to the dedication of the church on July 29, 1794, where he gave the opening sermon. Bethel was the first black Methodist church in the United States, and Frank was honored to be present at its dedication. In his journal he wrote gratefully, "Our colored brethren are to be governed by the doctrine and discipline of the Methodists."

On August 20, 1795, Frank turned fifty years old. By now his blond hair had turned gray, and his body was beginning to break down under the strain of constant travel. Somehow Frank still found the strength to ride a thousand or more miles every three months in all kinds of weather. Sometimes he was so weak that he had to be strapped to his horse so he could ride without falling off. On one occasion he was too ill to walk across a room but insisted that he get back on his horse and move along—others on the circuit were awaiting his arrival. The truth was that Frank hated to be restricted to staying in one place, especially when it meant he could not preach on a Sunday. He would call such a day "dumb Sabbath."

There were no dumb Sabbaths while out riding the circuits. And although he had no home of his own, Frank had a hundred homes scattered across America, as people kept a bed or a room ready for him in their houses or cabins. His journals and books, along with his few other belongings, were still stored at Perry Hall, and Frank enjoyed the times when he made it back to the Goughs' residence to stay. People on the Methodist circuits also watched out for Frank's needs. One woman had her seamstress make him a new suit of clothes every time he came to visit, while others would swap out his old, worn horse for a new one.

One thing that helped to ease Frank's burden a little occurred when the General Conference appointed a preacher to travel with him. This was a wonderful opportunity for Frank to pass along his insights on preaching, the Bible, spiritual life, and the affairs of the church. He spent hundreds of hours talking and praying with another preacher while their horses clopped along. Two of the men Frank discipled in this way as they accompanied him were William McKendree and Jesse Lee. Both men had second thoughts about aligning themselves with James O'Kelly, and Frank had encouraged them to come back into the Methodist fold. He was glad when they did, and as he rode with them, his conviction was confirmed that the Methodist Church in America would be the stronger for their return.

Frank continued to send his parents half of his salary, small as it was, and wrote to them as often as he could. He prayed for them regularly, especially since his parents were now in their eighties. Then in July 1798, Frank received word that his father had died two months before. He was sad to hear the news. For a moment he wondered whether he should send for his mother and bring her to the United States, but he quickly decided that this was not practical. Eliza Asbury was probably too weak by now to survive a crossing of the Atlantic Ocean by ship.

As the sun rose on January 1, 1800, at the dawn of a new century, Francis Asbury was in Charleston, South Carolina, officiating at a Methodist conference. Just three days later, he and the residents of Charleston learned that President George Washington had died on December 14, 1799. Charleston was stunned, and Frank recorded in his journal, "Washington, the calm, intrepid chief, the disinterested friend, first father, and temporal saviour of his country under divine protection and direction. . . . At all times he acknowledged the providence of God, and never was he ashamed of his Redeemer. We believe he died not fearing death. In his will he ordered the manumission [freeing] of his slaves, a true son of liberty in all points."

Four months later, at the General Conference in Baltimore on May 1, 1800, Frank planned to resign his position of superintendent. He felt old and worn-out and thought a younger man might be more suited to the job. But the conference delegates would not hear of

it. Instead they voted to appoint a third bishop in the
church—Richard Whatcoat. This was a great relief to
Frank, since Thomas Coke was often away attending
to other Methodist business. Following the death of
John Wesley, Thomas had become the secretary to the
English Conference of Methodists and was assigned
to oversee the expansion of Methodism into other
parts of the world. All of this kept him very busy, and
his visits to the United States were short. Richard was
spiritual, loyal, hardworking, a good friend, and committed to the growth of the Methodist Church in North
America. Frank knew that he could trust Richard to
gladly share the burden of administrative duties.

With the dawn of a new century came new challenges. By now the population of the United States
was over five million, but only one person in fourteen
belonged to any church. This, of course, did not escape
Frank's notice, and he looked for new ways to reach
the nation's growing population with the gospel.

By 1800 the Wilderness Road was wide enough
for wagons to travel, and thousands of people began
to migrate west, pouring over the passes and down
the Ohio River on huge rafts. As more and more set-
tlers moved onto the frontier, the Methodist work
continued to grow there. In October 1800, Frank traveled with Richard Whatcoat and William McKendree
(who had been ordained an elder and oversaw the
Methodist work on the western frontier). The men
made their way through the frontier areas, preaching and holding conferences as far west as Nashville,
Tennessee.

On the outskirts of Nashville the trio came upon a strange scene. Several hundred Presbyterians were holding a camp meeting at Drake's Creek Meetinghouse. Frank stopped to investigate. He learned that those attending the camp meeting had come from up to fifty miles away in their wagons, bringing with them tents and their own food. They had set up camp in a grove of trees near a spring. The men slept beneath the wagons, and the women and children in tents. At dawn a trumpet would sound to rouse the campers and call them to meetings that lasted all day and late into the night. Often there were between ten and thirty preachers all speaking at the same time in different spots around the camp. At first glance it seemed like chaos. Some people prayed aloud while others silently fell to their knees. Some yelled out praises and Bible verses, and wailing, laughter, and crying could be heard.

The camp meeting was more emotional and chaotic than anything Frank had seen before, but it did not shock him. In the midst of the chaos he saw God at work as Christians rejoiced in their faith or came under deep conviction of their sin and turned their lives over to the Lord. Frank was intrigued and confided in his journal, "This is fishing with a large net." What was needed, he was sure, was to take those enthusiastic new converts from the camp meeting and turn them into mature, evangelical Christians.

Frank saw that the Methodist framework was a perfect match for camp meetings. Methodist preachers were used to speaking outdoors to anyone who would listen, and the Methodist churches had a system in place to take new converts from camp meetings and disciple them. As a result, Frank began to encourage Methodist preachers to hold camp meetings for their circuits—not just those on the frontier but throughout the nation.

The camp meetings took off. Sometimes up to one thousand people came together for three or four days, occasionally up to seven days, to pray, listen to preaching and teaching, and just rejoice in their faith. Frank began attending these camp meetings whenever he could, preaching at them, studying them, and working with the local Methodist circuit riders to get the new converts into churches. As the preachers held camp meetings and followed up with the new converts, the number of Methodists in the country increased rapidly.

In April 1802, as camp meetings were becoming a fixture on Methodist circuits, Frank received word in Baltimore that his mother had died on January 2. He wrote a tribute to her in his journal: "For fifty years her hands, her house, her heart, were open to receive the people of God and ministers of Christ, and thus a lamp was lighted up in a dark place called Great Barr, in Great Britain."

Frank was now fifty-six years old, and his last tie with England had been severed. He was not sure he would live to be eighty-seven, as his mother had, but he was determined to use whatever time he had left to serve God and the Methodist cause.

Chapter 15

What Could He Do That He Did Not Do?

During the first five years of the new century, the United States was on the move. On March 1, 1803, Ohio became the seventeenth state in the Union. A little over a year later, on May 14, 1804, Meriwether Lewis and William Clark embarked on a journey west across the huge swath of land known as the Louisiana Territory. The United States had purchased the land from France the year before. The Lewis and Clark expedition hoped to travel across the entire North American continent to the Pacific Ocean, mapping the way for others to follow.

Around the same time, Francis Asbury wrote in his journal, "It is wonderful to see how Braddock's

Road is crowded with wagons and packhorses carrying families and their household stuff westward—to
the new state of Ohio, no doubt . . . here is a state
without slaves . . . and better for poor, hardworking
families. O highly favored land!"

While the United States was on the move, so too
was the Methodist Church. Frank described it as "like
a moving fire." Hundreds of people were responding
to the gospel at camp meetings across the country,
and during 1802 and 1803, Methodist membership
increased from 85,500 to 105,000 people. As the
denomination grew, dynamic young men stepped
forward to volunteer as circuit riders. Frank encouraged them, recalling his early days as a rider back in
England.

By now both Frank and Richard Whatcoat were
in frail health. Sometimes they traveled together,
urging each other on, stopping for various treatments and swapping horses so that the weaker one
could ride the steadier horse. Still, they were a team,
always moving among their people.

Bishop Thomas Coke had never enjoyed the endless circuit riding in the United States and instead
spent most of his time in England attending to Methodist business. In July 1805, Frank received a letter
informing him that at the age of fifty-eight, Thomas
had married a middle-aged heiress. Frank was pro-
foundly disappointed when he received the news. To
him, marriage and the family that went with it were
the number-one distraction for preachers. He wrote,
"I calculate we have lost the traveling labours of two

hundred of the best men in America, or the world, by marriage and subsequent location."

On those occasions when Thomas was present in the United States, almost no one recognized him by sight. By contrast, Bishop Francis Asbury was widely thought to be the most recognized person in the United States. More people recognized him than the president or any other public figure, including the late George Washington. This was due to Frank's relentless traveling and speaking. He stayed with people in log cabins as well as fine mansions and always sought someone to whom he could preach the gospel. Because of this, thousands of people claimed Frank as their spiritual father, and hundreds of babies were given the first names Francis Asbury. As Frank aged, many groups to whom he had preached wondered whether this would be the last time he would ride through their neck of the woods. People at the gatherings often wept when he arrived because they were so glad to see him. And they wept when he left because they believed they would never see him again.

Despite his age and illness, Frank felt compelled to go on, even though at times he was so sick he had to be carried into a meeting and placed in a chair at the altar. Sometimes his legs bothered him so much that he would preach on his knees—but preach he did, regardless of his condition. Frank noted in his journal, "They keep me busy. I must preach . . . some never expected to hear me again; possibly, I may never come again. I am reminded that such and such

I dandled in my lap. The rich, too, thirty years ago, would not let me approach them; now I must visit them and preach to them. And the Africans, dear, affectionate souls, bond and free, I must preach to them."

When he turned sixty years old in 1805, Frank began spending time planning for a smooth transition following his death. This process became more difficult when Richard Whatcoat died in July 1806. Frank mourned the loss of his fellow bishop and the memories they had shared. Frank had known Richard from his earliest days as a Methodist lad back in England. Richard's death again left Frank as the only bishop resident in the United States. If Frank died, there would be no bishop to take over the reins of the church.

This situation was remedied two years later when the 1808 General Conference voted to make William McKendree a bishop. Frank ordained him and with relief wrote, "The burden is now borne by two pairs of shoulders instead of one. The care is cast upon two hearts and two heads." Later he noted, "I wish the connection to do as well without me as with me, before they must do without me. I fret like a father who wishes to see his children married and settled before he dies."

During the 1808 conference Henry Gough died, and Frank took time out to preach at his funeral, which was attended by two thousand people. Frank remembered Henry with great fondness. He thought back on all the kindness the Goughs had bestowed on him over the years, how they had welcomed him to stay at Perry Hall and even kept a room set aside for him, and how Perry Hall had been a center for Methodist meetings in the area.

Frank now found that his circuit riding included visiting the graves of many of his old friends and circuit riders. He also visited many of the widows and children of preachers, encouraging them in the faith and making provision for them whenever he could.

In June 1812, war broke out between the United States and Great Britain. This time the war was fought mainly at sea, with the British navy blockading much of the Atlantic coast of the United States, the American-Canadian frontier around the Great Lakes and along the Saint Lawrence River, and the Gulf Coast. But Frank hardly noticed the war. His attention was firmly fixed on the Methodist circuits, which now involved his riding four thousand to six thousand miles a year to oversee.

On these travels, Frank especially loved meeting dedicated and daring young men like Richmond Nolley. Richmond was not much of a preacher, but because he loved to quietly encourage people in their faith, Frank assigned him to the remote Tombigbee region of Alabama. For two years Richmond rode from settlement to settlement, meeting with families in their homes and encouraging them in the Christian faith. One time while riding between settlements, Richmond noticed fresh wagon tracks leading up a streambed. He followed the tracks to a campsite, where he found a man, his wife, and their daughter.

The man was furious when he discovered that Richmond was a Methodist preacher. "What!" the man exclaimed. "How have you found me so soon? I left Virginia and Georgia just to get away from you. My wife and daughter are much attached to the Methodist practices, and I've been trying to get them away from your influence. And now here you are, finding us before our wagon is even unloaded!" Frank laughed aloud when Richmond told him the story. How wonderful it was to think that his preachers were going farther than any others.

Sometimes, though, Frank grieved over his preachers. On May 26, 1813, Frank preached at the funeral service of Robert Hibbard. Robert was a promising American who had been a preacher for four years. He offered himself as a missionary to Canada and was assigned to the Ottawa Circuit. While riding that circuit, he learned that the preacher assigned to his previous circuit in the United States had been called up to fight in the war against the British. Worrying about the spiritual state of his old friends, Robert set out from Ottawa to return to his old circuit to care for the spiritual needs of the people. While crossing the Saint Lawrence River on his way south, Robert drowned. It was a sad day for Frank as he preached at the funeral, but Frank took comfort in the fact that Robert had died serving his Master.

Frank started 1814 in North Carolina, and by February he had traveled north to Norfolk, Virginia, where he was laid up with illness. By March he felt well enough to press on to Maryland, traveling over icy, snow-covered roads. As the spring thaw began, Frank journeyed on through Delaware and Philadelphia, presiding over conferences, meeting with preachers, and exhorting Christian converts to follow the Methodist way. The truth was, though, that he was still very weak, so weak in fact that he did not write in his journal for three months. In July, Frank had the strength to cross the Appalachian Mountains once more, something he had now done over sixty times. On July 15 he mustered the strength to write in his journal: "I have been ill indeed, but medicine, nursing and kindness, under God, have been so far effectual that I have recovered strength enough to sit in my little covered wagon, into which they lift me." Then on July 19 he noted, "I look back upon a martyr's life of toil and privation and pain, and I am ready for a martyr's death."

In September Frank made it to Cincinnati, Ohio, for a conference. He learned that William McKendree had fallen from his horse and broken several ribs. Such was the lot of a circuit rider. Frank's own chest ached, and he began coughing up blood. He knew this was not a good sign for an old man, but he did not adjust his schedule. He had work to do, and he determined to be faithful to the end.

While Frank was in Cincinnati, stunning news arrived. American forces had been defeated in the Battle of Bladensburg, fought in Maryland three weeks before. British troops had entered Washington, DC, and burned many government buildings, including the president's mansion. Frank was saddened for the nation and for the destruction that war brought. He hoped that this chapter of American history would soon be over. He was certain that the Americans would eventually prevail, as they had done in the War of Independence. Of the British troops fighting the war, Frank noted in his journal, "They have no business here. Let them go home from whence they came. I shall pray against them with all my might. That is all I can do."

Despite the fact that he was coughing up blood, Frank continued on as best he could. When he was too ill to travel, he stayed with some of the thousands of friends he knew in every corner of the United States. Even when laid up with illness, he was never idle. He filled the time reading, answering mail, and praying.

In early 1815, good news spread across the country. In New Orleans the British had been soundly beaten by American troops under the command of General Andrew Jackson. The war with Great Britain appeared to be over. Frank, like most people in the country, rejoiced at the news.

In July 1815, Frank received news that Bishop Thomas Coke was dead. Thomas had set out for Ceylon, India, from England to escort seven Methodist missionaries there and help them set up a mission. He had died in his cabin on May 2, 1814, three weeks short of arriving in India. Thomas was buried at sea. At a memorial service for the bishop, Frank preached the sermon, declaring Thomas Coke to have been "a gentleman, a scholar, and a bishop to us, and as a minister of Christ, in zeal, in labours, in services—the greatest man in the last century."

The following month Frank turned seventy. He journeyed from South Carolina to attend the Ohio Conference. He now normally traveled in a small carriage, and a young preacher, John Wesley Bond, accompanied him on his journeys. Frank was grateful to have John at his side. John preached, helped Frank with his various medical treatments, and even carried him in and out of homes and meetinghouses when necessary. Sometimes, when Frank was too weak to be moved, he preached to crowds while sitting in his carriage. The people would gather around and sit on the ground, eager to hear from the man who had become a living legend. Even though Frank did not have children of his own, he was humbled to know that his "sons in the Lord" took care of him so well in his old age.

In Cincinnati, Ohio, Frank and William McKendree met together. Frank had spent many hours thinking about the way the West was opening up, and he was eager to ensure that the Methodist Church was on the forefront of the expanding nation. Frank summed up their meeting this way in his journal: "Bishop McKendree and [I] had a long and earnest talk about the affairs of our church and my future prospects. I told him my opinion was that the Western part of the empire would be the glory of America for the poor and pious; that it ought to be marked out for five Conferences, to wit: Ohio, Kentucky, Holston, Mississippi, and Missouri; in doing which, as well as I was able, I traced out lines and boundaries."

In October 1815, Francis Asbury gave up the last of his official responsibilities to William McKendree.

It was a bittersweet moment. "My eyes fail," he wrote on October 20, 1815. "I will resign the stations to Bishop McKendree; I will take away my feet. It is my fifty-fifth year of ministry and forty-fifth year of labor in America. My mind enjoys great peace and divine consolation."

A month and a half later, in early December, Frank set out from South Carolina in his carriage with John Wesley Bond at his side. They began making their way north toward Baltimore and the upcoming General Conference. On December 7, 1815, Frank noted in his journal, "We met a storm and stopped at William Baker's, Granby." It was the last entry Frank ever wrote in his journal.

Frank and John continued slowly on their way toward Baltimore, stopping at Methodist churches and homes along the way to preach. By now Frank's sermons were rambling, and he was in much pain as they rode.

On Sunday, March 31, 1816, Frank could go no farther. He and John were staying at the home of Joseph Arnold in Spotsylvania County, Virginia, when Frank collapsed. Frank was put to bed, where he grew weaker. He insisted that the Arnold family gather around his bed for worship, since it was Sunday morning. John read the daily reading from the Methodist prayer book: "And God shall wipe away all tears from their eyes; and there shall be no more death, neither sorrow, nor crying, neither shall there be any more pain: for the former things are passed away" (Rev. 21:4).

Later in the day Frank asked to sit in a chair. John lifted him from the bed into the chair and held his head up. Frank smiled and nodded. He then lifted both his arms heavenward and quietly died.

John Wesley Bond sent a messenger to announce the sad news to the Methodists of America: "Our dear father has left us and has gone to the church triumphant. He died as he lived—full of confidence, full of love—at four o'clock this afternoon."

Bishop Francis Asbury was buried in the Arnolds' family cemetery, but when the General Assembly met at the beginning of May, they arranged to have his body moved to Baltimore. Frank's funeral service was held on May 10, 1816. About twenty-five thousand people—black and white, old and young, educated and illiterate—walked silently behind his casket as it was carried from the Light Street Chapel to the Eutaw Street Church, where he was buried. It was a sight no one in Baltimore had ever before witnessed, but it was fitting for the man who had given his life to bring the Good News to the people of the United States of America.

When Frank arrived in the American colonies in 1771, the Methodist Church had six hundred members. Now, in 1816, the church had grown to 214,000 members, with seven hundred preachers riding circuits. One American in every forty was now a Methodist in the fast-growing country, and countless other people had been impacted by Methodist teachings and practices.

At Frank's memorial service at St. George's in Philadelphia, Ezekiel Cooper, one of Frank's preachers and a man who had known him for over thirty years, asked this question about Francis Asbury: "What could he do that he did not do? For he exhausted all his strength, broke down his constitution, spent his talents and his all, and wore out his life, for the good of man and for the glory of God."

Bilhartz, Terry D., ed. *Francis Asbury's America: An Album of Early American Methodism*. Grand Rapids: Zondervan, 1984.

Hallam, David J. A. *Eliza Asbury: Her Cottage and Her Son*. Studley, UK: Brewin Books, 2003.

Ludwig, Charles. *Francis Asbury: God's Circuit Rider*. Fenton, MI: Mott Media, 1984.

Nygaard, Norman E. *Bishop on Horseback: The Story of Francis Asbury*. Grand Rapids: Zondervan, 1962.

Rudolph, L. C. *Francis Asbury*. Nashville: Abingdon, 1966.

Salter, Darius L. *America's Bishop: The Life of Francis Asbury*. Grand Rapids: Francis Asbury Press, 2003.

Smeltzer, Wallace Guy. *Bishop Francis Asbury, Field Marshal of the Lord*. Denver: W. G. Smeltzer, 1982.

Story, Bettie Wilson. *Gospel Trailblazer: The Exciting Story of Francis Asbury*. Nashville: Abingdon, 1984.

Tipple, Ezra Squier, ed. *The Heart of Asbury's Journal*. New York: Eaton & Mains, 1904.

Wigger, John. *American Saint: Francis Asbury and the Methodists*. New York: Oxford University Press, 2009.

_____ *About the Authors*

Janet and Geoff Benge are a husband and wife writing team with more than twenty years of writing experience. Janet is a former elementary school teacher. Geoff holds a degree in history. Originally from New Zealand, the Benges spent ten years serving with Youth With A Mission. They have two daughters, Laura and Shannon, and an adopted son, Lito. They make their home in the Orlando, Florida, area.